Writing English

By the same authors

Explore and Express
An English Course for Secondary Schools
Book 1
Book 2
Book 3
Book 4

Using English
An English Examination Course

Writing English

Richard Adams Lord Williams's School, Thame
John L. Foster Lord Williams's School, Thame
Robert L. Wilson Aylesbury Grammar School

Macmillan Education

First published 1980

Published by
MACMILLAN EDUCATION LIMITED
Houndmills Basingstoke Hampshire RG 21 2 XS
and London
Associated companies in Delhi Dublin
Hong Kong Johannesburg Lagos Melbourne
New York Singapore and Tokyo

Printed in Hong Kong

British Library Cataloguing in Publication Data

Adams, Richard
Writing English.
1. English language – Composition and exercises
I. Title   II. Foster, John Louis   III. Wilson,
Robert Lewis
808'.042   PE1413

ISBN 0–333–25517–8

Contents

Introduction

This book is designed for use by students in colleges and in the upper forms of the secondary school. The aims of *Writing English* are to make students aware of the many different forms of writing which they encounter from day to day; to help students to recognise their special characteristics, to distinguish the subtleties of their modes of functioning, and to understand the proper occasions and circumstances in which they are used; and to develop the students' own skills in utilising them appropriately. The book consists of eight units, each dealing with a particular mode of writing. Each unit contains a number of pieces of writing, chosen both for study and to serve as models and as a stimulus for the students' own writing. In addition to discussion questions, designed to provide the students with insights into the writer's craft, his motives and his use of language; there are commentaries pointing out particular techniques, and exercises giving students the opportunity to practise their own writing skills. The units are self-contained and can, therefore, be used as appropriate within existing Advanced level, liberal studies and general English courses.

Acknowledgements

The authors and publishers wish to thank the following who have kindly given permission for the use of copyright material:

Edward Arnold (Publishers) Ltd for extracts from *Three Anti-Nazi Broadcasts* by E. M. Forster; Associated Book Publishers Ltd for an extract from 'The Militant Rambler' by Robert Lynd from *Rain, Rain, Go To Spain*, published by Methuen & Co. Ltd; The Bodley Head Ltd for an extract from *Ulysses* by James Joyce; Curtis Brown Ltd on behalf of Barry Hines for an extract from *Speech Day*; P. R. Brown for a review of 'Elidor' by Alan Garner from *The Times Educational Supplement*, 27 May 1977; Jonathan Cape Ltd on behalf of the Estate of F. R. Fletcher for extracts from *Kilvert's Diary*, edited by William Plomer; on behalf of the Executors of the Ernest Hemingway Estate for an extract from *A Farewell to Arms*; on behalf of Edward Albee for an extract from *Who's Afraid of Virginia Woolf?* and on behalf of the Estate of Robert Frost for 'Stopping By Woods On A Snowy Evening' and 'Acquainted With the Night' from *The Poetry of Robert Frost* edited by Edward Connery Lathem; Frank Cass & Co. Ltd for an extract from *D. H. Lawrence: A Personal Record* by E. T. (Jessie Chambers); Cassell Ltd for extracts from *The War Speeches* by Sir Winston Churchill; Constable & Co. Ltd for an extract from *Journal of Katherine Mansfield* by J. Middleton Murry; The Daily Telegraph Ltd for 'The Nasty Sound of Youth' by Peregrine Worsthorne; 'Ever Onward' by

Frank Johnson; and 'Tobacco Firms and Smokers Face New Curbs' by David Loshak from *The Daily Telegraph*; and for 'Can Our Spaceship Survive' by John Gribbin from *The Daily Telegraph Magazine*; M. Chris Dalglish for a letter published by *The Daily Telegraph*, 22 April 1978; Faber & Faber Ltd for an extract from *The Inheritors* by William Golding; Karenza Gardner for a review 'Bulldog Drummond at Bay, by Sapper' from *The Times Educational Supplement*, 27 May 1977; A. M. Heath & Co. Ltd on behalf of the Estate of George Orwell for an extract from 'The Sporting Spirit' from *Collected Essays, Journalism and Letters of George Orwell*, edited by Sonia Brownwell Orwell and published by Martin Secker and Warburg Ltd; David Higham Associates Ltd on behalf of Richard Adams and Robin Nelson for an extract from *It's A Crime*; and on behalf of the Trustees for the Copyrights of Dylan Thomas for an extract from *Twenty Years A-Growing*; The Hogarth Press on behalf of the Estate of Virginia Woolf for an extract from *To the Lighthouse*; Mrs Laura Huxley and Chatto & Windus Ltd for the essay 'Comfort' from *Proper Studies* by Aldous Huxley; IPC Magazines for an article 'It'll All Be U. S. To Us' by David Bradbury from the *Daily Mirror*, 28 June 1978; Jeremy Lack for a review 'Rosy Is My Relative' by Gerald Durrell from *The Times Educational Supplement*, 27 May 1977; Wendy Malpass for a letter 'Lack of Influence by Parents' from *The Sunday Telegraph*, 23 April 1978; John Murray (Publishers) Ltd for an extract from *The Court of Richard II* by Gervase Mathew; Oxford University Press for extracts from *Collected Letters of Wilfred Owen* by Harold Owen and John Bell; 'Riders to the Sea' from *Plays*, Book I, by J. M. Synge, edited by Ann Saddlemyer; and *Macbeth* by William Shakespeare, edited by Bernard Groom; Geoffrey H. Peake for a letter published in *The Sunday Telegraph*, 16 April 1978; Penguin Books Ltd for an extract from 'Pop Music' by Donald J. Hughes from *Discrimination and Popular Culture*, edited by Denys Thompson, (2nd Edition 1973) © Penguin Books 1966, 1973; Phaidon Press Ltd for extracts from *The Paintings* by Grunewald and an extract from *Trois Primitifs* by J. K. Huysmans; Laurence Pollinger Ltd on behalf of the Estate of Mrs Frieda Lawrence Ravagli for an extract from *Sons and Lovers* by D. H. Lawrence published by William Heinemann Ltd; Reuters Ltd for an article 'Britons and Americans are Growing Words Apart' published in *The Times*, 28 June 1978; Scottish Health Education Unit for extracts from *Understanding Alcohol and Alcoholism in Scotland* by Marquis Grant; Sidgwick & Jackson Ltd for an extract from *Travels* by Edward Heath; Times Newspapers Ltd for the article 'Cold Feet on Metrication' from *The Times Educational Supplement*, 19 May 1978; review 'Zig-Zag Matilda' by David Williams *The Sunday Times*, 19 February 1978; and the review 'Round the World in 80 Clichés' by Paul Theroux from *The Sunday Times*, 11 December 1977; Harvey Unna & Stephen Durbridge Ltd on behalf of Giles Cooper for extracts from the plays 'Mathry Beacon' and 'The Disagreeable Oyster'; Doreen M. Williams for a letter published in *The Sunday Telegraph*, 16 April 1978; Yale University Press for an extract from *The Pastoral Art of Robert Frost* by John F. Lynen.

The authors and publishers wish to acknowledge the following photograph sources:

BBC Copyright p. 112; D G Dine facing page 1; Giraudon/Musée d'Unterlinden, Colmar pp. 184/5; Graham Photography p. 22; David G Hodge p. 64; Mansell Collection pp. 170, 188 top; John Preece Photography p. 46; Syndication International pp. 92, 146; Victoria and Albert Museum p. 188 bottom; Young and Rubicam Limited pp. 136/7.

The Publishers have made every effort to trace the copyright holders but if they have inadvertently overlooked any, they will be pleased to make the necessary arrangements at the first opportunity.

I   Prose fiction

Fact or fiction?

People sometimes write or talk as if – from a literary point of view – fact and fiction are entirely unrelated concepts. This is, however, far from the truth. The best writers of all types of so-called fictional literature derive much of the impact and authenticity of their work from a faithful observation of human behaviour and a close analysis of their own personal experiences. The characters about which they write may be largely imaginary, but the situations in which they find themselves, the relationships and emotions they share – all have the reality and truth of life.

This sort of close interweaving of fact and fiction can best be illustrated by comparing a passage from D. H. Lawrence's novel *Sons and Lovers* with an extract from the memoir written by Jessie Chambers about her friendship with the writer. When you have studied these pieces, consider carefully the questions which follow them as a preparation for the writing exercise with which the section concludes.

And he, coming home from his walks with Miriam, was wild with torture. He walked biting his lips and with clenched fists, going at a great rate. Then, brought up against a stile, he stood for some minutes, and did not move. There was a great hollow of darkness fronting him, and on the black up-slopes patches of tiny lights, and in the lowest trough of the night, a flare of the pit. It was all weird and dreadful. Why was he torn so, almost bewildered, and unable to move? Why did his mother sit at home and suffer? He knew she suffered badly. But why should she? And why did he hate Miriam, and feel so cruel towards her, at the thought of his mother? If Miriam caused his mother suffering, then he hated her – and he easily hated her. Why did she make him feel as if he were uncertain

I

of himself, insecure, an indefinite thing, as if he had not sufficient sheathing to prevent the night and the space breaking into him? How he hated her! And then, what a rush of tenderness and humility!

Suddenly he plunged on again, running home. His mother saw on him the marks of some agony, and she said nothing. But he had to make her talk to him. Then she was angry with him for going so far with Miriam.

'Why don't you like her, mother?' he cried in despair.

'I don't know, my boy,' she replied piteously. 'I'm sure I've tried to like her. I've tried and tried, but I can't – I can't!'

And he felt dreary and hopeless between the two.

Spring was the worst time. He was changeable, and intense and cruel. So he decided to stay away from her. Then came the hours when he knew Miriam was expecting him. His mother watched him growing restless. He could not go on with his work. He could do nothing. It was as if something were drawing his soul out towards Willey Farm. Then he put on his hat and went, saying nothing. And his mother knew he was gone. As soon as he was on the way he sighed with relief. And when he was with her he was cruel again.

One day in March he lay on the bank of Nethermere, with Miriam sitting beside him. It was a glistening, white-and-blue day. Big clouds, so brilliant, went by overhead, while shadows stole along on the water. The clear spaces in the sky were of clean, cold blue. Paul lay on his back in the old grass, looking up. He could not bear to look at Miriam. She seemed to want him, and he resisted. He resisted all the time. He wanted now to give her passion and tenderness, and he could not. He felt that she wanted the soul out of his body, and not him. All his strength and energy she drew into herself through some channel which united them. She did not want to meet him, so that there were two of them, man and woman together. She wanted to draw all of him into her. It urged him to an intensity like madness, which fascinated him, as drug-taking might.

He was discussing Michael Angelo. It felt to her as if she were fingering the very quivering tissue, the very protoplasm of life, as she heard him. It gave her her deepest satisfaction. And in the end it frightened her. There he lay in the white intensity of his search, and his voice gradually filled her with fear, so level it was, almost inhuman, as if in a trance.

'Don't talk any more,' she pleaded softly, laying her hand on his forehead.

He lay quite still, almost unable to move. His body was somewhere discarded.

'Why not? Are you tired?'

'Yes, and it wears you out.'

He laughed shortly, realizing.

'Yet you always make me like it,' he said.

'I don't wish to,' she said, very low.

'Not when you've gone too far, and you feel you can't bear it. But your unconscious self always asks it of me. And I suppose I want it.'

He went on, in his dead fashion:

'If only you could want *me*, and not want what I can reel off for you!'

'I!' she cried bitterly – 'I! Why, when would you let me take you?'

'Then it's my fault,' he said, and, gathering himself together, he got up and began to talk trivialities. He felt insubstantial. In a vague way he hated her for it. And he knew he was as much to blame himself. This, however, did not prevent his hating her.

One evening about this time he had walked along the home road with her. They stood by the pasture leading down to the wood, unable to part. As the stars came out the clouds closed. They had glimpses of their own constellation, Orion, towards the west. His jewels glimmered for a moment, his dog ran low, struggling with difficulty through the spume of cloud.

Orion was for them chief in significance among the constellations. They had gazed at him in their strange, surcharged hours of feeling, until they seemed themselves to live in every one of his stars. This evening Paul had been moody and perverse. Orion had seemed just an ordinary constellation to him. He had fought against his glamour and fascination. Miriam was watching her lover's mood carefully. But he said nothing that gave him away, till the moment came to part, when he stood frowning gloomily at the gathered clouds, behind which the great constellation must be striding still.

There was to be a little party at his house the next day, at which she was to attend.

'I shan't come and meet you,' he said.

'Oh, very well; it's not very nice,' she replied slowly.

'It's not that — only they don't like me to. They say I care more for you than for them. And you understand, don't you? You know it's only friendship.'

Miriam was astonished and hurt for him. It had cost him an effort. She left him, wanting to spare him any further humiliation. A fine rain blew in her face as she walked along the road. She was hurt deep down; and she despised him for being blown about by any wind of authority. And in her heart of hearts, unconsciously, she felt that he was trying to get away from her. This she would never have acknowledged. She pitied him.

from 'Sons and Lovers' by D. H. Lawrence

I spent the morning with mother and the small children, feeling still a little spent after the strain and excitement of the examination days. In the front garden the clumps of narcissi stood in shadowed stillness. I began to expect Lawrence soon after midday, but the afternoon passed, and when at last he wheeled his bicycle through the big yardgate he was not the Lawrence of the night before.

'You said you were coming early,' I reproached him. He made no answer and avoided my glance. When tea was over he suggested that we should read some French and we went into the stackyard and sat on a log beside the hay-stack. Our dog Trip, a big white bull-terrier, came up to us with doggish delight and lay at our feet. To my surprise Lawrence drove him away:

'Go away, Trip,' he said. 'We don't want you, you're not nice.'

We read a little, but soon Lawrence closed the book and began to speak in a strained voice.

'This . . . this friendship between us . . . is it keeping even . . . is it getting out of balance, do you think?'

My mind barely grasped his words. It was his voice that warned me.

'I think it is keeping in balance,' I replied, bewildered. 'I don't know what you mean.'

'I was afraid,' he went on, as if the words had to be forced out, 'that the balance might be going down on one side. You might, I

4

thought, I don't know, you might be getting to care too much for me.'

I felt my heart turn cold, and replied:

'I don't think so. I haven't thought about it.'

He was silent.

'But why are you saying this?' I asked in deep dismay.

'Well, they were talking last night, mother and E. E. asked mother if we were courting.' He spoke with difficulty. 'They say we either ought to be engaged or else not go about together. It's the penalty of being nineteen and twenty instead of fifteen and sixteen,' he concluded bitterly.

I began to understand.

'Ah – I always thought your mother didn't like me,' I said quietly.

'It isn't that, you mustn't think that; mother has nothing against you,' he urged. 'It's for your sake she spoke. She says it isn't fair to you . . . I may be keeping you from getting to like someone else. She says I ought to know how I feel,' he went on painfully. 'I've looked into my heart and I cannot find that I love you as a husband should love his wife. Perhaps I shall, in time. If ever I find I do, I'll tell you. What about you? If you think you love me, tell me, and we'll be engaged. What do you think?'

The world was spinning around me. I was conscious of a fierce pain, of the body as well as of the spirit. I tried not to let him see my tears. As clearly as if in actuality I saw the golden apple of life that had been lying at my fingertips recede irretrievably. We sat for some moments in an ashen silence.

When I could speak I told him with truth that I had not thought about love, and that anyhow I couldn't become engaged under such circumstances. He made a movement as though some obstacle was cleared out of the way. A blankness came over me and I had to make an effort to attend to what he was saying in a lifeless voice.

'Very well then, we'll decide what we're to do.'

'There's nothing to decide,' I said. 'We'll have nothing to do with one another.'

'No,' he said with decision, 'we shall have something to do with one another. We have so much in common, we can't give it all up. Mother said we needn't give everything up, only we must know what footing we're on, that's all. Life isn't so rich in friendship that we can afford to throw it away. And this is the only friendship that's ripened,' he ended pathetically.

I maintained that there was no footing at all, it would be better to drop everything. But he would not hear of it.

'No, we shall not. We shall not give everything up. It means too much to us. We can't give it all up. There's the question of writing, we want to talk about that. And there's the French, we can go on reading together, surely? Only we'll read in the house, or where they can see us. And chapel, that's important. You must keep on coming, and I'll ask Alan not to cycle and then he can walk home with us. And when we go down the fields we'll take the youngsters with us. We needn't let people think we're on a different footing from what we are, that's all. Only we must go on talking to one another.'

I listened in silence, stunned and indifferent. He had evidently come up with the plan all worked out. Presently he asked, miserably:

'Will you tell your mother?'

I replied that I should not.

'Shall I tell them, then?' he said.

'No,' I answered, my tears getting the better of me. 'They'd be awfully angry and tell you never to come again.'

He turned and looked at me with wide, distraught eyes, and I said:

'It has nothing to do with them. I manage my own affairs.'

We sat a little while in silence and misery, with the dusk coming on. When we went into the house mother exclaimed:

'Why, Bert, is something the matter? You're so white. You've sat out there and got cold.' Then to me: 'You shouldn't let him sit out like this, you ought to think.'

I made no answer and Lawrence said:

'I'm all right.'

He sat on the sofa, looking painfully white. The children's painting-box lay open on the table. Lawrence glanced at it, then took a sheet of paper from an exercise book and wrote briefly. He handed the paper to me and I read:

'The children's painting-box needs replenishing. Who will subscribe? I open the list. D.H.L., 1s.'

Soon he said he would go home. Ordinarily I should have gone with him to the barn to fetch his bicycle and open the gate, but I drew the two small children on to my lap. At the window Lawrence turned and gave me an unforgettable look. I clung to the children and we began to sing the humorous ballads they were so fond of. Mother said, 'I'm sure there's something wrong with Bert, he's so white. And why has he gone home so early?'

I was glad that my sister was not sharing my bedroom that night. I could not have endured anyone to know the humiliation I suffered, and the sense of irreparable loss. For I realized that life was completely changed, that there could never be the same sympathy between us again, so deep that it was unconscious. I knew, too, that a cruel injury had been done to young life; the delicate fabric of our relationship had been mutilated deliberately. The issue of love in its crudest sense had been forced upon us while we were still immature and unprepared. I felt that it was a cruel stroke designed to kill what was only in process of formation. In a letter to me five years later Lawrence described it as 'the slaughter of the foetus in the womb'.

from 'D. H. Lawrence; A Personal Record' by E.T. (Jessie Chambers)

1   What close resemblances can you detect between the characters and circumstances of the extract from *Sons and Lovers* and those mentioned in Jessie Chambers's memoir? Are there any strong dissimilarities?

2   What particular role do the mothers (Paul's and Lawrence's) play in the two situations? Is the mother-son relationship brought out more fully in either one?

3   In which of the two passages is the mother figure viewed the more sympathetically? Can you suggest why this might be?

4   Look closely at the first paragraph of the extract from *Sons and Lovers*. What special stylistic features does it contain? Are they evidenced elsewhere in the extract? Are there any moments of similar intensity in Jessie Chambers's account? What conclusions can you draw from a comparison of the two passages on stylistic grounds?

5   Write an episode or short story in which — though composing a fiction — you base incident and character alike on your own personal experiences.

Narrative styles

In narrative fiction one of the author's primary aims is to convey insights into the emotions of the characters about whom he is writing. To do this he may choose to write in great detail about the characters and their reactions, and about the setting in which an event takes place, using imagery and symbol to help extend the reader's understanding of the characters' feelings. Alternatively, he may describe an event in a very direct way, including only the essential details, yet nevertheless, by his skilful selection and arrangement of those details, enable the reader to see beneath the surface of the event and thus to perceive exactly what the characters are feeling.

The following two extracts are contrasting examples of these different styles of writing. Whereas Lawrence includes a great amount of detail, carefully chosen to create an impression of the intensity of the feelings of the two characters, Hemingway writes in a restrained style, giving a very simple, matter-of-fact description of the events. Throughout the passage the emotions of the characters are constantly understated, yet the reader is made aware of the depths of their feelings.

Lad-and-girl love

In this further extract from D. H. Lawrence's novel *Sons and Lovers*, Paul Morel and Miriam Leivers are walking home together one summer evening.

One evening in the summer Miriam and he went over the fields by Herod's Farm on their way from the library home. So it was only three miles to Willey Farm. There was a yellow glow over the mowing-grass, and the sorrel-heads burned crimson. Gradually, as they walked along the high land, the gold in the west sank down to red, the red to crimson, and then the chill blue crept up against the glow.

They came out upon the high road to Alfreton, which ran white between the darkening fields. There Paul hesitated. It was two miles home for him, one mile forward for Miriam. They both looked up the road that ran in shadow right under the glow of the north-west sky. On the crest of the hill, Selby, with its stark houses and the up-pricked headstocks of the pit, stood in black silhouette small against the sky.

He looked at his watch.

'Nine o'clock!' he said.

The pair stood, loth to part, hugging their books.

'The wood is so lovely now,' she said. 'I wanted you to see it.'

He followed her slowly across the road to the white gate.

'They grumble so if I'm late,' he said.

'But you're not doing anything wrong,' she answered impatiently.

He followed her across the nibbled pasture in the dusk. There was a coolness in the wood, a scent of leaves, of honeysuckle, and a twilight. The two walked in silence. Night came wonderfully there, among the throng of dark-trunks. He looked round, expectant.

She wanted to show him a certain wild-rose bush she had discovered. She knew it was wonderful. And yet, till he had seen it, she felt it had not come into her soul. Only he could make it her own, immortal. She was dissatisfied.

Dew was already on the paths. In the old-oak wood a mist was rising, and he hesitated, wondering whether one whiteness were a strand of fog or only campion-flowers pallid in a cloud.

By the time they came to the pine-trees Miriam was getting very eager and very intense. Her bush might be gone. She might not be able to find it; and she wanted it so much. Almost passionately she wanted to be with him when he stood before the flowers. They were going to have a communion together – something that thrilled her, something holy. He was walking beside her in silence. They were very near to each other. She trembled, and he listened, vaguely anxious.

Coming to the edge of the wood, they saw the sky in front, like mother-of-pearl, and the earth growing dark. Somewhere on the outermost branches of the pine-wood the honeysuckle was streaming scent.

'Where?' he asked.

'Down the middle path,' she murmured, quivering.

When they turned the corner of the path she stood still. In the wide walk between the pines, gazing rather frightened, she could distinguish nothing for some moments; the greying light robbed things of their colour. Then she saw her bush.

'Ah!' she cried, hastening forward.

9

It was very still. The tree was tall and straggling. It had thrown its briers over a hawthorn-bush, and its long streamers trailed thick right down to the grass, splashing the darkness everywhere with great split stars, pure white. In bosses of ivory and in large splashed stars the roses gleamed on the darkness of foliage and stems and grass. Paul and Miriam stood close together, silent, and watched. Point after point the steady roses shone out of them, seeming to kindle something in their souls. The dusk came like smoke around, and still did not put out the roses.

Paul looked into Miriam's eyes. She was pale and expectant with wonder, her lips were parted, and her dark eyes lay open to him. His look seemed to travel down into her. Her soul quivered. It was the communion she wanted. He turned aside, as if pained. He turned to the bush.

'They seems as if they walk like butterflies, and shake themselves,' he said.

She looked at her roses. They were white, some incurved and holy, others expanded in an ecstasy. The tree was dark as a shadow. She lifted her hand impulsively to the flowers; she went forward and touched them in worship.

'Let us go,' he said.

There was a cool scent of ivory roses — a white, virgin scent. Something made him feel anxious and imprisoned. The two walked in silence.

'Till Sunday,' he said quietly, and left her; and she walked home slowly, feeling her soul satisfied with the holiness of the night. He stumbled down the path. And as soon as he was out of the wood, in the free open meadow, where he could breathe, he started to run as fast as he could. It was like a delicious delirium in his veins.

from 'Sons and Lovers' by D. H. Lawrence

1 How do Paul and Miriam feel as they stand on the crest of the hill? What details mentioned in the first two paragraphs does Lawrence include in order to heighten the impression of their feelings that he wishes to convey?

2 How do their feelings differ as they walk towards the wood? What is the significance of the snatch of conversation that is included?

3 Why does Miriam want Paul to go into the wood and what does the rose bush symbolize for her?

4   The details that Lawrence mentions of the woodland scene help to extend the reader's awareness of Miriam's and Paul's emotions. How do (a) Miriam's (b) Paul's feelings develop and change as they walk towards the bush? Which details that Lawrence includes help you most to understand what they are feeling?

5   What do they experience as they stand before the rose bush together? How do their feelings differ as they do so and afterwards, as they make their way home? What details that Lawrence includes in his description of the rose bush and of the way they stand before it and then make their way home, help to reveal their emotions?

6   Summarise what the experience meant to Miriam and what it meant to Paul. Re-read the passage and list the words and phrases, and the details that helped you to understand a) Miriam's and b) Paul's feelings.

Catherine

The following extract from Ernest Hemingway's *A Farewell to Arms* occurs at the very end of the novel where, following the loss of her baby at birth, Catherine is desperately ill in hospital.

The nurse opened the door and motioned with her finger for me to come. I followed her into the room. Catherine did not look up when I came in. I went over to the side of the bed. The doctor was standing by the bed on the opposite side. Catherine looked at me and smiled. I bent over the bed and started to cry.

'Poor darling,' Catherine said very softly. She looked grey.

'You're all right, Cat,' I said. 'You're going to be all right.'

'I'm going to die,' she said, then waited and said, 'I hate it.'

I took her hand.

'Don't touch me,' she said. I let go of her hand. She smiled.

'Poor darling. You touch me all you want.'

'You'll be all right, Cat. I know you'll be all right.'

'I meant to write you a letter to have if anything happened, but I didn't do it.'

'Do you want me to get a priest or anyone to come and see you?'

'Just you,' she said. Then a little later, 'I'm not afraid. I just hate it.'

'You must not talk so much,' the doctor said.

'All right,' Catherine said.

'Do you want me to do anything, Cat? Can I get you anything?'

Catherine smiled. 'No.' Then a little later, 'You won't do our things with another girl, or say the same things will you?'

'Never.'

'I want you to have girls, though.'

'I don't want them.'

'You are talking too much,' the doctor said. 'You cannot talk. Mr. Henry must go out. He can come back again later. You are not going to die. You must not be silly.'

'All right,' Catherine said. 'I'll come and stay with you nights,' she said. It was very hard for her to talk.

'Please go out of the room,' the doctor said. Catherine winked at me, her face grey. 'I'll be right outside,' I said.

'Don't worry, darling,' Catherine said. 'I'm not a bit afraid. It's just a dirty trick.'

'You dear, brave sweet.'

I waited outside in the hall. I waited a long time. The nurse came to the door and came over to me. 'I'm afraid Mrs. Henry is very ill,' she said. 'I'm afraid for her.'

'Is she dead?'

'No, but she is unconscious.'

It seems she had one haemorrhage after another. They couldn't stop it. I went into the room and stayed with Catherine until she died. She was unconscious all the time, and it did not take her very long to die.

Outside the room in the hall I spoke to the doctor. 'Is there anything I can do tonight?'

'No. There is nothing to do. Can I take you to your hotel?'

'No, thank you. I am going to stay here a while.'

'I know there is nothing to say. I cannot tell you – '

'No,' I said. 'There's nothing to say.'

'Good night,' he said. 'I cannot take you to your hotel?'

'No, thank you.'

'It was the only thing to do,' he said. 'The operation proved – '

'I do not want to talk about it,' I said.

'I would like to take you to your hotel.'

'No, thank you.'

He went down the hall. I went to the door of the room.

'You can't come in now,' one of the nurses said.

'Yes, I can,' I said.

'You can't come in yet.'

'You get out,' I said. 'The other one too.'

But after I had got them out and shut the door and turned off the light it wasn't any good. It was like saying good-bye to a statue. After a while I went out and left the hospital and walked back to the hotel in the rain.

   from 'A Farewell to Arms' by Ernest Hemingway

7 How much detail is included about Catherine's appearance and about the hospital room?

8 What are Mr. Henry's feelings while he is in the room with his wife, while he waits outside and as he is with her while she is dying? How do you know what he is feeling?

9 How does Hemingway convey to the reader what Mr. Henry feels after his wife's death?

10 What are the main differences between Hemingway's style and Lawrence's style? Do you find that one is more successful than the other in conveying characters' emotions or are they equally effective in different ways?

Stream of consciousness

Around the beginning of this century a new style of narrative prose writing emerged which has come to be known as 'stream of consciousness'. The author, instead of focusing his attention on a sequence of events and watching his characters react to them, attempts to enter into the minds of his characters and to see external events from behind their eyes. He is more concerned with all the multifarious thoughts and feelings that may flash through the mind in a very short time than he is with the way one action leads on from another and in turn produces various results for different people. In 'stream of consciousness' literature the writer's point of view has shifted: he does not see his characters from a distance; he endeavours to come close to whatever they are aware of in any one moment, however insignificant that particular moment may appear to be.

The reason why such a style of writing should have emerged in this century is related to the major changes that have occurred in our way of thinking about the nature of experience. Instead of having firm religious beliefs and settled values, we are, generally speaking, far more uncertain about life and its meaning than people said they were in, for example, the Victorian age. Writers have responded to this change by emphasising the potential richness of each changing moment. Virginia Woolf, one of the most influential writers of the early part of the twentieth century, expressed this idea in her essay *Modern Fiction*:

Examine for a moment an ordinary mind on an ordinary day. The mind receives a myriad impressions — trivial, fantastic, evanescent, or engraved with the sharpness of steel. From all sides they come, an incessant shower of innumerable atoms; and as they fall, as they shape themselves into the life of Monday or Tuesday, the accent falls differently from of old.

(a) All the characters mentioned in the following extract are staying in the Ramsay's holiday home in Skye. They are preparing to make a visit by boat on the following day to a remote lighthouse and Mrs Ramsay is at the moment knitting a pair of long socks for the lighthouse keeper's little boy. She measures the sock against the leg of her own son James to see if it is long enough and, as she does so, a great variety of thoughts and observations pass through her mind.

'And even if it isn't fine tomorrow,' said Mrs Ramsay, raising her eyes to glance at William Bankes and Lily Briscoe as they passed, 'it will be another day. And now,' she said, thinking that Lily's charm was her Chinese eyes, aslant in her white, puckered little face, but it would take a clever man to see it, 'and now stand up, and let me measure your leg,' for they might go to the Lighthouse after all, and she must see if the stocking did not need to be an inch or two longer in the leg.

Smiling, for an admirable idea had flashed upon her this very second — William and Lily should marry — she took the heather mixture stocking, with its criss-cross of steel needles at the mouth of it, and measured it against James's leg.

'My dear, stand still,' she said, for in his jealousy, not liking to serve as measuring-block for the Lighthouse keeper's little boy, James fidgeted purposely; and if he did that, how could she see, was it too long, was it too short? she asked.

She looked up — what demon possessed him, her youngest, her cherished? — and saw the room, saw the chairs, thought them fearfully shabby. Their entrails, as Andrew said the other day, were all over the floor; but then what was the point, she asked herself, of buying good chairs to let them spoil up here all through the winter when the house, with only one old woman to see to it, positively dripped with wet? Never mind: the rent was precisely twopence half-penny; the children loved it; it did her husband good to be three thousand, or if she must be accurate, three hundred miles from his library and his lectures and his disciples; and there was room for visitors. Mats, camp beds, crazy ghosts of chairs and tables whose London life of service was done — they did well enough here; and a photograph or two, and books. Books, she thought, grew of themselves. She never had time to read them. Alas! even the books that had been given her, and inscribed by the hand of the poet himself: 'For her whose wishes must be obeyed' . . . 'The happier Helen of our day' . . . disgraceful to say, she had never read them. And Croom on the Mind and Bates on the Savage Customs of Polynesia ('My dear, stand still,' she said) neither of those could one send to the Lighthouse. At a certain moment, she supposed, the house would become so shabby that something must be done. If they could be taught to wipe their feet and not bring the beach in with them — that would be something. Crabs, she had to allow, if Andrew really wished to dissect them, or if Jasper believed that one could make soup from seaweed, one could not prevent it; or Rose's objects — shells, reeds, stones; for they were gifted, her children, but all in quite different ways. And the result of it was, she sighed, taking the whole room from floor to ceiling, as she held the stocking against James's leg, that things got shabbier and shabbier hot summer after summer. The mat was fading; the wallpaper was flapping. You couldn't tell any more that those were roses on it. Still, if every door in a house is left perpetually open, and no lockmaker in the whole of Scotland can mend a bolt, things must spoil. What was the use of flinging a green Cashmere shawl over the edge of a picture frame? In two weeks it would be the colour of pea soup. But it was the doors that annoyed her; every door was left open. She listened. The drawingroom door was open; the hall door was open; it sounded as if the bedroom doors were open; and certainly the window on the landing was open, for that she had opened herself. That windows should be open, and doors shut — simple as it was, could none of them remember it? She would go into the maids' bedrooms at night and find them sealed like ovens, except for Marie's, the Swiss girl, who would rather go without a bath than without fresh air, but then at home, she had said, 'the mountains are so beautiful'. She had said that last night looking out of the window with tears in her eyes. 'The mountains are so beautiful.' Her father was dying there, Mrs Ramsay knew. He was leaving them fatherless. Scolding and demonstrating (how to make a bed, how to open a window, with hands that shut and spread like a Frenchwoman's) all had folded itself quietly about her, when the girl spoke, as, after a flight through the sunshine the wings of a bird fold themselves quietly and the blue of its plumage changes from bright steel to soft purple. She had stood there silent for there was nothing to be said. He had cancer of the throat. At the recollection — how she had stood there, how the girl had said 'At home the mountains are so beautiful', and there was no hope, no hope whatever, she had a spasm of irritation, and speaking sharply, said to James:

'Stand still. Don't be tiresome,' so that he knew instantly that her severity was real, and straightened his leg and she measured it.

from 'To the Lighthouse' by Virginia Woolf

1 Examine this passage and take note of all the references to the actual event taking place. How frequently does Virginia Woolf remind us of the simple action, the measuring of the stocking? How long do you think it took, longer or shorter than the time it takes to read the passage?

2 Review the thoughts that pass through Mrs Ramsay's mind. Are they all of the same type? Which thoughts are related to the people she notices around her and to the room she is in at this moment? Which thoughts recall memories from her recent or more distant past? Does she think of the future at all?

3 What impression of Mrs Ramsay's personality do you gain from this extract? Take into account the way she reacts to other people, their opinion of her and the sort of concerns that fill her mind.

4 How much do you learn about the circumstances of Mrs Ramsay's life, about the holiday home in which they are staying, her family and friends?

(b) James Joyce's monumental novel, *Ulysses*, covers the actions and thoughts of three main characters during one day. In this novel, the external events, the sequence of action during the day, is, on the whole, less trivial and inconsequential than the action of *To the Lighthouse* and the thoughts of the characters are very often more intertwined with what they are doing. One might say that for much of the novel the stream of consciousness flows more intermittently than it does in Virginia Woolf's novel. Consider the following passage from the early chapters of *Ulysses*.

Mr Leopold Bloom ate with relish the inner organs of beasts and fowls. He liked thick giblet soup, nutty gizzards, a stuffed roast heart, liver slices fried with crustcrumbs, fried hencod's roes. Most of all, he liked grilled mutton kidneys which gave to his palate a fine tang of faintly scented urine.

Kidneys were in his mind as he moved about the kitchen softly, righting her breakfast things on the humpy tray. Gelid light and air were in the kitchen but out of doors gentle summer morning everywhere. Made him feel a bit peckish.

The coals were reddening.

Another slice of bread and butter: three, four: right. She didn't like her plate full. Right. He turned from the tray, lifted the kettle off the hob and set it sideways on the fire. It sat there, dull and squat, its spout stuck out. Cup of tea soon. Good. Mouth dry. The cat walked stiffly round a leg of the table with tail on high.

—Mkgnao!

—O, there you are, Mr Bloom said, turning from the fire.

The cat mewed in answer and stalked again stiffly round a leg of the table, mewing. Just how she stalks over my writing-table. Prr. Scratch my head. Prr.

Mr Bloom watched curiously, kindly, the lithe black form. Clean to see: the gloss of her sleek hide, the white button under the butt of her tail, the green flashing eyes. He bent down to her, his hands on his knees.

— Milk for the pussens, he said.

— Mrkgnao!' the cat cried.

They call them stupid. They understand what we say better than we understand them. She understands all she wants to.

Vindictive too. Wonder what I look like to her. Height of a tower? No, she can jump me.

—Afraid of the chickens she is, he said mockingly. Afraid of the chookchooks. I never saw such a stupid pussens as the pussens.

Cruel. Her nature. Curious mice never squeal. Seem to like it.

—Mrkrgnao! the cat said loudly.

She blinked up out of her avid shameclosing eyes, mewing plaintively and long, showing him her milkwhite teeth. He watched the dark eyeslits narrowing with greed till her eyes were green stones. Then he went to the dresser, took the jug Hanlon's milkman had just filled for him, poured warmbubbled milk on a saucer and set it slowly on the floor.

—Gurrhr! she cried, running to lap.

He watched the bristles shining wirily in the weak light as she tipped three times and licked lightly. Wonder is it true if you clip them they can't mouse after. Why? They shine in the dark, perhaps, the tips. Or kind of feelers in the dark, perhaps.

He listened to her licking lap. Ham and eggs, no. No good eggs with this drouth. Want pure fresh water. Thursday: not a good day either for a mutton kidney at Buckley's. Fried with butter, a shake of pepper. Better a pork kidney at Dlugacz's. While the kettle is boiling. She lapped slower, then licking the saucer clean. Why are their tongues so rough? To lap better, all porous holes. Nothing she can eat? He glanced round him. No.

In quietly creaky boots he went up the staircase to the hall, paused by the bedroom door. She might like something tasty. Thin bread and butter she likes in the morning. Still perhaps: once in a way.

He said softly in the bare hall:

—I am going round the corner. Be back in a minute.

And when he had heard his voice say it he added:

—You don't want anything for breakfast?

A sleepy soft grunt answered:

—Mn.

from 'Ulysses' by James Joyce

1 What does Mr Bloom do in the course of this extract? What impression of his character is conveyed?

2   Pick out some moments in which Joyce slips, as it were, into Mr Bloom's mind. How does he convey an effect of the immediacy of snatches of thought? Is this the way people really think? Consider also the range of thinking that occupies Bloom. What different topics occur to him?

3   Compare the use of the stream of consciousness technique in these two passages. Do Joyce and Virginia Woolf use it for precisely the same purposes? To what extent is depth of character revealed in either passage?

(c) A quite different effect is achieved by William Golding in *The Inheritors*. This novel presents a group of primitive Neanderthal people and explores the way they react to the coming of the more intelligent and advanced *homo sapiens* into their tribal area. For much of the novel we actually view its events through the eyes of the primitive people. They have no comprehension of the skills and thought that the more advanced tribe have developed. They record what they see without understanding it. The main character is Lok and, in the following extract, he is looking out over a river at one of the new people who is hiding in the bushes on the opposite bank.

The bushes twitched again. Lok steadied by the tree and gazed. A head and chest faced him, half-hidden. There were white bone things behind the leaves and hair. The man had white bone things above his eye and under the mouth so that his face was longer than a face should be. The man turned sideways in the bushes and looked at Lok along his shoulder. A stick rose upright and there was a lump of bone in the middle. Lok peered at the stick and the lump of bone and the small eyes in the bone things over the face. Suddenly Lok understood that the man was holding the stick out to him but neither he nor Lok could reach across the river. He would have laughed if it were not for the echo of the screaming in his head. The stick began to grow shorter at both ends. Then it shot out to full length again.

The dead tree by Lok's ear acquired a voice.

'Clop!'

His ears twitched and he turned to the tree. By his face there had grown a twig: a twig that smelt of other, and of goose, and of the bitter berries that Lok's stomach told him he must not eat. This twig had a white bone at the end. There were hooks in the bone and sticky brown stuff hung in the crooks. His nose examined this stuff and did not like it. He smelled along the shaft of the twig. The leaves on the twig were red feathers and reminded him of goose. He was lost in a generalized astonishment and excitement.

from 'The Inheritors' by William Golding

1   What can you deduce about the appearance of Lok and the appearance of the new man from this passage?

2   What is the new man doing? Try to interpret all those details that, at first reading, may seem obscure in this passage.

3   Lok clearly does not understand the intentions of the new man. Which details in the passage show him as trying to make sense out of what is happening?

Here are three methods of organising your own writing by employing stream of consciousness techniques:

1   Think of a brief and simple action performed by one person. Then think of what the character might be aware of, from his past and present and anticipations of the future. Try to convey the circumstances in which your character finds himself and the sort of person he is as you present his thoughts and feelings within the framework of one ordinary moment in his day.

2   Describe someone in action and, at the same time, convey the thoughts of the character. Move in and out of the character's mind in the way that Joyce does in the second extract.

3   Lok's comprehension of events in the passage from *The Inheritors* is similar to that of a young child surrounded by adults doing things that he cannot understand. Develop a piece of description from the point of view of a character who does not understand what is going on around· him. Try to limit your vocabulary to the sort of words the character might himself use.

2 Summaries

Making summaries — whatever we may feel when confronted with them in class or in examinations — is by no means an arid academic exercise. It is indeed closely related to the process we naturally adopt when we pass on the main gist of some complicated message to a friend, when we outline the plot of a book or a film for the benefit of someone who wishes to investigate it for himself, or even when we make our own mental note of the matters which are of interest to us from a rapid general survey of the daily news — whether in the papers or on the radio or television. Summary work of any description requires a number of important skills: it requires first insight — the ability to see clearly and accurately to the heart of the material under scrutiny; it also requires judgement — the capacity to weigh up which aspects of the original are of primary importance as opposed to those which may be safely omitted without distorting the theme or argument; and it requires a ready appreciation of the aim and intention of the original together with the integrity to retain these in the summary version.

Today's student is commonly confronted with two main types of summary. There is that which is sometimes referred to as 'précis', where an entire passage has to be reduced to about one-third of its original length and where all the main points have to be covered. The other type is that in which the student is required to pick out information about one aspect of the topic under discussion and to present a reasoned digest of only that material which is directly relevant. From a play-extract, for instance, he may be required to summarise the main features embodied in a particular character; from an article or essay, the information which supports just one side of the argument.

It is useful, in approaching the writing of summaries of both these types, to bear in mind the following rules and procedure:

1   Read the extract quickly in order to identify its purpose and the general direction of its argument. Then reread it (more than once if necessary), observing its structure and the way in which the author carries through his intentions. By the end of your reading, you should have a thorough grasp of the meaning of the extract. It is useful at this

stage to try summing up the point of the extract in a single sentence or even in the form of a title.

2 When this preparatory work is complete, note down the main points of the argument. In this, you will find that the paragraph division of the original is very often a helpful guide, working on the principle that one of the basic rules of sound writing is the allocation to a separate paragraph of each new point in the discussion. Try, therefore, to deduce the central idea of each paragraph.

3 Put away the original text and, with the aid of your notes and your memory, make a rough summary of the argument. Write as if the statements you are making are your own; do not, that is, employ devices of reported speech like 'the author says . . .' or 'he then goes on to insist that . . .' Avoid the inclusion of unnecessary minor details such as lists of examples or illustrations.

4 Go over your rough draft with the original beside you, ensuring that all the principle points are adequately covered, that the correct emphasis is maintained, that the author's intentions are carried through accurately and that the theme or argument of the original is in no way distorted.

5 Polish your corrected draft. Make sure that it is in good continuous English prose and that it avoids excessive quotation from the original. It is not strictly necessary to observe the paragraph divisions of the original piece. Your summary should, on the other hand, aim to reflect the style of the original; an essay written in serious, scientific language, for example, should be summarised in a similar tone, not in — say — the popular colloquial idiom.

6 With all your corrections and stylistic adjustments complete, write out a neat final version.

*

1 Here is a passage from a book about the life and times of King Richard II. Carry out the first two steps in the procedure for summarising outlined above: that is, read and reread the passage and devise for it a short title or sentence of explanation. Then, taking each paragraph in turn, make notes on the main points of the argument.

By 1385 an elaborate court was fully functioning and life within it was conditioned by the preferences of the King. It is possible to know Richard II more intimately than any other medieval English Sovereign. He was tall; when his skeleton was examined in 1871 it was found to be nearly six feet high. His thick dark yellow hair fell heavily to his shoulders. He had a pale white skin which probably flushed easily. He remained cleanshaven later than was customary, perhaps to prolong his look of adolescence. Later in the 1390s he was elaborately barbered, with tufts of beard on either side of his chin and a slight moustache at the extremities of his lips, but even then at times he returned to being fully shaved. The zest with which he had himself portrayed suggests that he was convinced of his own beauty. He was physically brave. He showed a rash courage on several occasions: at Smithfield in 1381, and when he rode into Bolingbroke's camp at Flint in 1399, and perhaps in 1397 when he went in person to arrest his uncle Thomas at Pleshey. Three times he led his army in the field. But unlike his father and his grandfather he never jousted. This is curious, for he had an interest in horseflesh, and sent four envoys to Prague to improve his stud from the Luxemburg stables. Perhaps unlike his father and his grandfather he would have found it insufferable to be unhorsed. It may have been part of his conception of the royal dignity that as King he could preside at tournaments but not take part in them. He was passionate in his friendships but perhaps fickle in them. He had a long memory for injuries. He was given to sudden gusts of violent anger, but it is likely that when he wished he had considerable charm which he expressed demonstratively. He delighted in giving great grants of land, new offices and titles: he invented the rank of Marquess for Robert de Vere and later created the Marquessage of Dorset; and he made five new Dukes in 1397.

A prodigal generosity ('largesse') and the quality of being physically rash ('outrageus') were both highly prized among the upper class of his time. But Richard had two traits which must have caused mistrust: it is certain that he was recklessly careless of his pledged word, and probable that he usually planned several moves ahead. The easiest explanation of his reign is that, like John of Gaunt but unlike the Black Prince, he played life as if it were chess, not draughts. He was defeated not because he was a bad chess-player but because he had taken too many calculated risks.

Three of his tastes affected the whole character of his court; he cared for books; he was devoted to fine and exotic cooking; and he was passionately interested in dress.

It is exceedingly improbable that Richard ever knew any of the classics but it is likely that they formed part of his conception of good letters. In 1395 he commissioned a Latin epitaph for his tomb in Westminster Abbey and in it he had himself compared to Homer ('Omerus'). He may well have savoured the list of names in Chaucer's poems: Virgil and Ovid and Lucan, Statius and Claudian. His two vernaculars were French and English. When he was thirteen he bought a *Romance of the Rose* and romances of Gawain and of Perceval and a Bible in French. Since he paid £28 for them they must have been manuscripts de luxe. Later he was to keep books in his private closet and this suggests that he could read as well as listen. Nineteen of these were rebound between 1386 and 1388: their covers were of red satin or of blue and white satin; their markers and their fastening strings were of blue silk; some had gold clasps. It is possible that his taste had been influenced by that of his tutor Sir Simon Burley, who owned ten romances in 1387, nine in French and one in English. But he also had a desire for novelties. We know from the dedication of the *Confessio Amantis* that he had commissioned John Gower to write him 'some newe thing'. In this he may have been affected by the literary fashions of the Valois court; his friend John de Montacute, Earl of Salisbury, wrote French poems which were admired in the circle of Christine de Pisan. The association between the court and the new literary movements was made possible by Richard's liking for books.

The nature of the court feasts was determined by his interest in fine cooking and the zest for new combinations of contrasting flavours. His court cookery book *The Forme of Cury* has been preserved: the manuscript came into the possession of the Staffords, was presented by Edmund Stafford to Queen Elizabeth and later was part of the Harleian Collection; it was printed for the Society of Antiquaries in the reign of George III. It is stated in its prologue that Richard is accounted 'the best and ryallest vyander of all Christian Kings' and that the book is compiled by his master cook with the 'assent and avysement of maisters of phisik and of philosophie' that dwelt in his court. It consists of 196 recipes, and throughout there is an emphasis on the exotic; the recipe for cooking oysters in Greek wine seems characteristic. A considerable luxury trade is presupposed: spices are in common use; there is much pepper, sometimes whole, sometimes powdered, and much ginger; there are frequent references to cinnamon, cardamom, nutmeg and saffron and in one case to spikenard; sugar of Cyprus seems specially prized, but there is also white sugar and sugar clarified with wine. During these years there were close trade contacts between Genoa and Southampton, and it is likely that the far-eastern spices were brought by Genoese ships from Trebizond and from Caffa in the Crimea. Although there is an obvious delight in the use of costly ingredients, *The Forme of Cury* does not suggest the excess of Georgian banquets. The recipes fall naturally into three courses: there were 'potages', main dishes, and 'sotiltees' which were either sweets or savouries. A characteristic potage is venison broth; a typical sotiltee is the 'moree', mulberries cooked with honey. The 'mawmenee' may be chosen to represent the main courses: it had a basis of minced flesh of pheasant, to which Greek wine, cinnamon, cloves and ginger were added and then two pounds of sugar. Sugar and spice are combined frequently. In another main dish the basis is provided by shelled oysters; these were cooked in wine together with rice, ginger, sugar and mace.

There is no reference to the haunches of venison, the loins of beef, the mutton or the roasted ox which might be expected at a medieval feast and which probably featured often enough at the dinner of a country magnate. At Richard's court, meat does not seem to have been served whole at table: there are directions as to how it should be 'teysed' or 'morterysed' before being cooked, and the main course must often have resembled a gigantic pâté. Hare's flesh was a common basis of such pâtés, but one of them was constructed from deers' livers cooked in wine. All this suggests that in the court circle men and women eat with spoons, not with their hands. It would seem that the sotiltees at the end of the meal were intended to appeal also to the eye. At times they were carefully shaped and directions are given as to their colouring; saffron, or red, or 'jaulnas' which is orange-tawny.

Remote Italian influences seem to have been fashionable. In *The Forme of Cury* 'Lumbard Mustard' is a favoured condiment and olive oil is often used in place of butter. Rhenish wine was drunk and wine from La Rochelle, but there are frequent references to Vernage, a strong white wine from Northern Italy. Perhaps zabaglione is the only surviving dish that Richard would have savoured. A novel interest in the intricacies of the art of cooking

27

was a mark of the international court culture of the late fourteenth and early fifteenth centuries and was to be a legacy to Europe.

Possibly Richard valued the recipes of his Master Cook for their elaborate and modern elegance. He may have had a similar reaction to the creations of his Master Tailor, Walter Raufe. It would seem inconceivable that Richard ever considered himself to be vain, but possible that he thought of himself as proud. In the 1390s vanity in dress was recognised as the expression of 'superbia'. On the south wall of the nave of the church of Brooke in Norfolk there is a painting of Superbia as a young man with waved hair and crowned with roses; he is elaborately dressed and girdled, and is gazing at a looking-glass which he holds in his right hand while in his left hand he holds a double comb. On the north side of the nave at Hoxne in Suffolk, Superbia is a richly dressed young man with bell-mouthed sleeves, holding in one hand a sceptre and in the other a looking-glass. Both wall-paintings have been dated between 1390 and 1400.

It seems clear that it was Richard's intense interest in his own dress that was responsible for the extravagant and quickly changing fashions of his court. In the new court milieu tailoring at last developed into an art. This is a point first made by the author of *Richard the Redeless*, who records the reactions of the town middle class in the autumn of 1399.

But now ther is a gyse: the queyntest of alle
A wondir coriouse crafte: come now of late
That men clepith kerving.

He asserts that a tailor might now charge twenty times the cost of his material. He describes the courtier who carried his whole fortune on his body and who in order to win a Duke's praise feared no debt and begged and borrowed from the town burgesses:

And douteth no dette: so dukes hem preise
And begith and borwith: of burgeis in tounes.

A whole section of his poem has as one of its texts 'qui mollibus in domibus regum sunt'.

Court dress seems first to have become magnificent in the early years of Richard's personal rule. In 1388 Sir Simon Burley owned a tabard of cloth-of-gold embroidered with roses and lined with green tartarine, a scarlet tabard embroidered with the sun and with golden letters, a white leather coat embroidered with the Burley badge of the Stakes and ornamented with fifty-four gold buttons, an ermine cape and a cloak of pure minever. Such display was financially possible since rich dress was portable capital and money could be raised in its security. In 1387 and 1388 Simon Burley had raised money from six London citizens on the security of his clothes and of his beds.

from 'The Court of Richard II' by Gervase Mathew

Here now are two précis of this passage. By careful reading and reference to the original, decide which the more closely answers to the rules for summarising mapped out at the beginning of the unit. The following questions may be helpful in making your decision:

(a) Which précis shows the clearer insight into Gervase Mathew's argument and the more accurately reflects his intentions?

(b) Make a detailed comparison of the first two paragraphs of the original with the first three of précis A and the first two of précis B and comment on the fidelity with which the two summarisers have approached their task.

(c) Which précis more nearly observes the rule about omitting unnecessary detail? Is there any point in the argument where illustration is essential to full understanding?

(d) Which summary comes closer to the length (one-third of that of the original) usually suggested for exercises of this kind?

(e) Does either précis fall short on stylistic grounds? Examine their paragraphing. Which do you rate to be the more satisfactory from this point of view?

When you have decided which précis you consider the better try improving on it and polishing it further and then comparing your work with that of other members of your set or class.

(a) By 1385, Richard's court was flourishing, its life conditioned by the likes and dislikes of the king.

Richard was tall, almost six feet high, with thick dark yellow, shoulder length hair. His pale white skin probably flushed easily and he remained clean shaven later than most men of the age. In

1390s he displayed tufts either side of his chin with a slight moustache at the ends of his lips, and took such care with the way he portrayed himself to suggest he was convinced of his own beauty. He was physically brave, demonstrating his courage on several occasions including the meeting with Bolingbroke at Flint and three times leading his army into battle. However, despite this and unlike his forefathers, Richard took no active part in jousting, preferring simply to preside at tournaments. He was passionate but often deceitful in his friendships and had a long memory for injuries. He was prone to violent outrage but could demonstrate considerable charm when he wished, and delighted in appointing new offices and titles or giving great grants of land.

Although the qualities of generosity and being physically rash were highly prized at the time, Richard was very careless with his pledged word and probably planned things several moves ahead which must have created a certain air of mistrust.

The character of Richard's court was affected by three of his tastes; his care for books, his devotion to exotic cooking and his passionate interest in dress.

It is unlikely that Richard knew any of the classics in any detail but thought enough of them to have himself compared with Homer in his epitaph. That Richard later kept books in his private closet suggests that he could read as well as listen. He seemed to love romances and may well have been influenced in this respect by his tutor Sir Simon Burley who owned ten of them. He also encouraged novel forms of writing, commissioning John Gower to write 'some newe thing' for him. In this he may have been influenced by the Valois court and his friend John de Montacute. The introduction of new forms of literature into his court was made possible by Richard's liking for books.

Richard's interest in fine and exotic cooking determined the nature of the court feasts. 'The Forme of Cury', his court cookery book, has been preserved and is found to contain 196 recipes with a strong emphasis on the exotic. Spices and other flavourings were widely used which implies there was a considerable luxury trade at the time. The recipes were divided into three main courses: firstly 'potages', a typical example being venison broth, main dishes such as minced pheasant flesh doused with wine and spices, and finally 'sotiltees' such as 'moree' – mulberries cooked with honey.

There is no mention of great joints of meat being roasted and served such as we might expect at a medieval feast. Instead, meat seems to have been served as a gigantic pâté, suggesting that the men and women of the court ate with spoons and not their hands. It also appears that the 'sotiltees' were intended to be nice to look at as well as to eat, since special instructions are given for their shape and colouring.

This novel interest in the art of cooking was a mark of European court culture around the turn of the fourteenth century.

Richard loved elaborate cooking and he probably valued the work of his Master tailor in the same sort of way. At this time vanity in dress was regarded as the expression of 'superbia'. Superbia became a richly dressed character who symbolised vanity and deceit. Richard probably thought himself more as just proud.

Richard's intense interest in his own dress was clearly responsible for the extravagant court fashions at the time. Magnificence in court dress really coincided with the first few years of Richard's reign. For the court, rich dress was really portable capital which could be used as security to raise money when required.

(b) Life within his court was much influenced by the king's personal tastes. We know more about Richard II than any other medieval king: tallish, with dark yellow hair offsetting his pale skin, he was – for most of his adult life – cleanshaven, and he seems to have had a high regard for his own beauty. Though he displayed conspicuous personal bravery several times during his life, on the battlefield as elsewhere, he appears never to have taken an active part in jousting tournaments. In matters of enmity and friendship he was a man of extremes, his sudden bursts of anger contrasting vividly with his great charm and love of giving extravagant presents. His generosity and his physical rashness were qualities much prized among his peers. Two further characteristics, however – his carelessness over honouring promises and his tendency to take calculated risks – are likely to have aroused mistrust among Richard's contemporaries.

Three of his particular interests shaped the taste of his court: books, the art of cookery and fashionable dress.

Richard is unlikely to have been closely acquainted with the classics but he probably recognised their value as part of the complete literary study. His native tongues were French and English. From an early age he took an interest in collecting finely bound manuscripts and books written in the former language. He also appreciated novelties, however, and is known to have commissioned the writing of new works. His interest fostered the new literary movements of his reign.

From Richard's court cookery book, which has been preserved, we know of his taste for fine cooking. Though they incline towards the exotic, the recipes in it also claim to have been approved on medical and philosophical grounds. In spite of a good deal of emphasis on luxury items, such as rare spices and sugars, the meals described appear to be relatively modest in scale, with three basic courses: a soup or broth, a main course of meat or fish, and finally a sweet or savoury. The common notion of a medieval feast based on an inexhaustible supply of roasts and joints is quite mistaken if Richard's court banquets are taken as the norm. There, the main courses seem to have been composed of dishes in which the meat was minced or pulped into a paste which was eaten with spoons. The last course of the meal was notable for the care taken over its presentation in matters of shaping and colouring. Italian influences of one sort or another were present in the development of cooking at Richard's court. There, as elsewhere in Europe, an interest in the fine details of the art established a fashion which has been handed on to later generations.

Richard's interest in new developments in cookery had its counterpart in a taste for the latest fashions in tailoring. Contemporary illustrations depict Pride as a well-groomed, richly-attired – sometimes princely – young man taking pleasure in the magnificence of his own appearance. The extravagant and rapidly changing fashions in dress at court seem to have derived directly from Richard's own inclinations in the matter. Tailors – sometimes to the distaste of the bourgeoisie – from being merely craftsmen became the recognised practitioners of an art, while their creations were so costly and were valued so highly that it was not uncommon for loans to be raised on the security of a courtier's wardrobe.

*

2 Let us trace some of the origins of modern popular music.

Over the years there have developed two different traditions in music. One is what we call 'art music', or (wrongly) classical music. In this the composer puts down his ideas on paper as exactly as possible, and the duty of the performer is to give as accurate an interpretation as he can of what the composer wrote, playing the 'correct' notes in the 'correct' time.

On the other hand, there is a tradition of popular music, or, as it is more commonly called, folk music, which has somewhat different characteristics. First of all, and fundamentally, the popular music tradition is an aural one. Tunes are handed down from one singer to another, and often change in the process. A singer may take liberties with a tune, may alter the notes or the rhythm, may purposely attack a note below pitch (as blues singers often do). There are some accepted common habits of performance, and an instrumentalist will harmonize a tune by ear with certain conventional and well-worn patterns of chords.

The two traditions have not always been as far apart and as clearly differentiated as they are today. It is of course only since music began to be written down in accurate notation that the extended compositions of the classical writers have been possible; and even up to the time of Handel and Mozart in the eighteenth century a good deal of improvisation took place in the performance of art music. But, as time went on, the two streams diverged more sharply. As every aspect of life became more prone to specialization, the composer of art music became more and more a professional writing for an educated audience, mainly aristocratic or middle-class, and more out of touch with the peasant or factory worker. In England, the folk tradition itself lost a great deal of its hold on everyday life because the old communities were broken up and destroyed by the Industrial Revolution; and it was only about 1900 that Cecil Sharp and others began to collect and to attempt to breathe a new life into the old folk-songs and dances. But while we owe them an incalculable debt for rescuing a great many lovely tunes which might otherwise have been lost, they did not always sufficiently realise that the old order in which this music had flourished had changed, and that much of it was irrelevant to a new society.

It was about the same time as this that jazz was making its first appearance in and around New Orleans. Many influences went to the making of jazz; but nearly all of them stemmed from the popular tradition – the Negro's songs of oppression, the dances of the Spaniards, and the African rhythms brought via the West Indians. Only the brass band music could be called partially an influence from the tradition of Western written music; and indeed the regular four-in-bar underlying pulse and the simple harmonic structures of the band marches were among the most important European elements in jazz. But it was by borrowing these and using them in the context of the popular tradition, with a great deal of improvisation, that the early jazz performers developed their characteristic music.

Jazz, in its traditional form at least, is true folk music. It has all the qualities listed above as typical of folk music and distinct from art music; and it is well known that many traditional players – not merely the amateurs – cannot read music.

It is true that in its modern style jazz is much less of a spontaneous improvised music. Controversy reigns as to whether commercial-style, big band music is true jazz; purists are commonly scathing about the claims of compositions like Gershwin's 'Rhapsody in Blue' to be considered jazz, and the intellectual and somewhat grandiose conceptions in which modernists such as Stan Kenton imitate some of the contemporary composers like Stravinsky are even more uncertainly designated as jazz.

Nevertheless no living means of artistic expression stands still. There is always development, and inevitably the original form of free-and-easy traditional jazz has been followed by many changes, most of which have been in the direction either of a larger grouping of instrumentalists or of more complex and sophisticated harmonies – both of which lead away from the true popular style and demand written arrangements and trained, rehearsed musicians.

Yet at the same time it is true that, whether it be mainstream or modern, or just plain commercial, you can usually trace the origin of each number to one or other of the two basic traditional jazz forms – the blues, with its lazy, dragging rhythm, its set harmonic

34

structure and its characteristic nostalgic note of oppression or of the frustrated search for the unattainable; or alternatively the high-spirited, noisy brashness of the four-in-a-bar quickstep rhythm, deriving from the old band marches, enlivened by the syncopating improvisations of generations of Negro jazz musicians.

Thus the development of jazz, as seen in the big bands of Duke Ellington and the commercial swing combinations of the thirties, and equally by the small 'chamber' groups, is natural and proper. Many may still prefer the spontaneity and the uninhibitedness of traditional jazz, with its simple sequences of well-used chords and its insistence on improvisation by the melody instruments; but this is not to deny to the other manifestations the name of jazz. No one can listen to the Modern Jazz Quartet or the Dave Brubeck Quartet, for example, without realising that the music has in it the essence of the jazz spirit. In both groups the drummer will create just that beat, whether it be the relaxed withheld swing of the slow blues tempo, or the exciting onward thrust of the quick movements, which is one of the hallmarks of good jazz. The curious and fascinating combinations of sound which both quartets derive from their choice of instruments may be far removed from the unsophisticated trumpet, clarinet or saxo-phone; and the chord progressions may contain a good deal of the chromatic harmonies of the late nineteenth century art music and be less instinctive and more worked out. But the quality and spirit are undeniably the quality and spirit of jazz.

But there is one particular feature of the original jazz which is of special interest to us. Because this music belongs to the tradition of music handed down aurally, music which is not put into permanent written form before performance, its underlying pattern must be basically simple. Thus, we have the blues form with its established formula of a twelve-bar sequence of chords. The strict blues always keeps to this pattern of chords; it is a most restricted form, and it is amazing how much variety has been obtained within it. It is a formula which is ideal for its purposes of aurally improvised music. Every singer and performer knows the harmonic pattern and feels it instinctively through long famili-arity; thus they can improvise freely within the framework. On the other hand, the rigidity of the scheme makes it unsuitable for large-scale development. It is not surprising that no-one has ever written a successful 'blues' symphony. 'Rhapsody in Blue' does not use the normal blues formula, and in any case its great weakness is its scrappiness, its lack of cohesion. It is equally true that few of the art composers of the written tradition have successfully produced large-scale compositions using folk melodies. Once again we see that the essential characteristics of folk and popular music are spontaneity and immediacy, as opposed to the long span of most art music, where one of the most important things is to be able to remember what happened two or three minutes ago, and to relate it to what you are hearing now.

It is the same with the 'quickstep' numbers, as I have rather arbitrarily chosen to call them. Take an old favourite like 'Alexander's Ragtime Band', and note how on a recording by the traditional New Orleans team led by Bunk Johnson the number consists of seven or eight variations improvised over the basic harmonic pattern of the tune — no development occurs, and no contrasting material is introduced; the formula is as simple as that of the blues, and as appropriate for the purpose.

I have emphasised this aspect of the essential simplicity of form of all traditional and most other jazz because it has an important bearing on the commercial popular music – the 'pop' music – which to a large extent has grown from it. Let us now turn to a further consideration of this music.

from 'Recorded Music' by Donald Hughes (from 'Discrimination and Popular Culture', ed. by Denys Thompson)

The following questions are for discussion and are designed to help you understand the passage printed above and to define those elements in it which you need to bring out in your summary.

1 Define clearly the central subject of the piece.

2 What is the purpose of the distinction between 'art music' and folk music? Is it essential to include this distinction in your summary?

3 Distinguish the 'many influences that went into the making of jazz'. Could you summarise them in a single sentence?

4 What are the two basic traditional jazz forms? How can we tell whether more recent music is within the mainstream of the jazz tradition?

5 To what extent is this author concerned to present an argument? To what extent is he concerned to narrate a sequence of occurrences, that

is, to write a history? If you think that both these elements are present, consider how the author combines them.

6   Write a summary of this passage reducing it to no more than a third of its original length.

*

3   The advent of the space age, and in particular the pictures of the Earth brought back by Apollo astronauts, has brought home to many people just how small our planet is on a cosmic scale. This has produced the concept of 'Spaceship Earth' as a description of our planet, and the concept is a good one. Like a spaceship, we have only finite resources to draw upon, and maintaining the air that we breathe, the water we drink and the food that we eat depends upon the efficient running of a recycling system which is not infallible and could be drastically affected by pollution if man's activities get out of hand.

Many people fear that such pollution of our life-support systems is now almost inevitable. The 'Prophets of Doom', as they have been called, suggest that over-population and continued wasteful use of natural resources may soon place such a strain on the systems of Spaceship Earth that starvation and disease could run riot, leaving few survivors to pick among the exhausted remains of our planet.

More recently, an equally extreme but almost diametrically opposed view has gained publicity. Professor Herman Kahn and others, who might well be labelled the 'Prophets of Boom', foresee a drastic reduction in human population – perhaps as a result of nuclear war – with the survivors building the golden age of mankind out of the ruins, using technology efficiently and maintaining population at 'sensible' levels.

These are the two extreme views, and both cannot be right. Indeed, the most probable future for Spaceship Earth must lie somewhere between the two extremes, with mankind achieving stability without suffering from a catastrophe first. In such a world, supporting 15 000 million people, our cities would have grown to form one global conurbation, with intensive agriculture and water purification plants covering the rest of the land surface.

It is possible to paint a picture now of what it would be like to live in such a world, and that picture is strikingly reminiscent of what some science fiction writers were telling us ten and even twenty years ago. But this picture is, like the science fiction worlds of the future, not the only possible future for Spaceship Earth. In particular, it takes no account of outside influences which might, as we shall see, change the situation significantly.

Whatever happens, if there is to be any future at all for mankind, the population of our planet – the 'crew' of Spaceship Earth – must be stabilised as quickly as possible. With child mortality now greatly reduced among even the poorest people on Earth, almost half of the people in the developing countries are younger than eighteen. So even if an ideal, 100 per cent effective contraceptive were introduced tomorrow and births were restricted to two in each family, there would still be an enormous population explosion, as these young people marry and have their own children.

And of course there is no prospect of such a super contraceptive being introduced worldwide tomorrow. If it is introduced in 1975, world population will stabilise, in about a hundred years, at 15 000 million – four times the present level. If it takes twenty years more to develop an ideal form of birth control, the stable population will be close to 20 000 million.

Professor Constantinos Doxiadis, a Greek regional planner who now works for the United Nations, has used just these figures in working out one possible scenario for the future of Spaceship Earth. He has assumed a stable population of between 15 000 and 19 000 million for the world of the mid-twenty-first century – but the distribution of this population, according to Doxiadis, would be far different from that of present-day society.

The only way in which such a vast population could be supported is by strict control and optimum use of all available land area. Farmlands would be just that: great areas devoted to food production, operated by automatic machinery and the few absolutely vital human overseers. And the cities of the world would have grown to form one giant conurbation, a world city in which people live packed together almost like battery hens. Villages and small towns would disappear. The growth of the cities of the world into one sprawling spiderweb would be along rivers and inland lakes in the continuing search for water, until, with a population of 15 000 million, natural water supplies are exhausted. Perhaps one-third of the world's land surface would then be needed for water collection and purification, with great pipelines carrying the precious liquid to the city.

But there is another liquid on which our civilisation depends – oil. As the events of last winter made clear, our technological world depends on power, and at present that means on oil. There seems little doubt that a world of 15 000 million people depending on technology to supply even their drinking water would need enormous supplies of fuel, far greater than the Earth's oil resources.

Nuclear power, of course, is the answer to these problems – at least it is according to the nuclear scientists. At the US Nuclear Research Center at Oak Ridge a plan has been developed to supply the energy needs of a population of 15 000 million. This involves a network of nuclear power stations floating on artificial islands in the world's oceans. Preliminary work on this project is already in hand, and Westinghouse plan to have the first 'floating nuclear park' operating off New Jersey in about six years' time.

The snag with nuclear fission power plants, however, is that they produce radioactive waste products, and a surfeit of these could alone be sufficient to make Spaceship Earth uninhabitable. But there is a real prospect of producing nuclear fusion reactors within a hundred years, operating on the same principle as the Sun itself. This would provide virtually unlimited energy, with very little radiation hazard. Whatever we hear about the merits of heavy water, fast breeder or other forms of fission reactors for the next twenty or thirty years it is fusion power which must eventually be called upon as the basic energy source.

Tapping of such a basic source of power also opens the way for recycling of raw materials. The technical ability to sort out the rubbish produced by a town and use it once again already exists, but worldwide recycling of all waste products would involve lavish use of power.

Of course, recycling only delays the day when all natural resources are exhausted, since the process is never 100 per cent effective. But given a few centuries of breathing space, which efficient recycling would allow, man may be able to go outside Spaceship Earth to bring in supplies from other planets. And further development of nuclear science could, if sufficient power is available, fulfil the alchemists' dream of transmutation of the elements on an industrial scale.

So it is possible to provide even a population of 15 000 million with power, water and room to live – although all three may be in short supply. That leaves the problem of food production.

It is already possible to produce synthetic food, and it is also possible to turn protein from the humble soya bean into a passable imitation of steak. But this does not necessarily mean that man will no longer grow other foods in a hundred years' time, even though the farms will be rather different from those of today.

The hydroponic food industry, which grows food plants without the inconvenience of using soil, is already starting up in the USA. At the University of Arizona, Tucson, vegetables are grown in large plastic tents, where a suitable 'climate' is maintained throughout the year. The plants can be suspended in a plastic mesh or placed in gravel beds, where all their nutrient requirements are supplied.

The results of the Tucson experiments have been so successful that a company has been formed to put the system into commercial production. And in Abu Dhabi a plastic covered hydroponic farm is being built to supply the sheikhdom with a million kilograms of vegetables a year. With this kind of technique, and, again, with the proviso that sufficient power is available to run the new food production systems, even 20 000 million people might be fed adequately.

So the message for mankind is that collapse of our civilisation is not inevitable, provided action is taken immediately to sort out the present mess Spaceship Earth is in. But the image of Spaceship Earth does have one flaw: there is one unjustified assumption underlying these visions of a stable future world supporting perhaps 20 000 million people adequately.

Although it might seem, on the scale of man's activities, that the Earth is a self-contained environment, that is not really the case. The very shape of the magnetosphere which forms the outer 'hull' of Spaceship Earth is distorted and moulded by outside influences. And the Earth must be regarded as one small component of the Solar System rather than as an independent spaceship in its own right.

from 'Can Our Spaceship Survive?' by John Gribbin .

1   Does the writer foresee a bright or a bleak future for the planet Earth? List the important factors that he thinks will ultimately decide whether or not our 'spaceship' survives.

2   You are the assistant features editor of a magazine. The article has been submitted for your consideration. You have been given ten minutes to produce your comments on it. Study and make notes on the article, then join up with a partner and take it in turns to tell each other what the main points of the article are.

3   You have been asked to write a description of the article for the Contents page of the magazine in which it is to appear. Your summary must not be more than three sentences long.

4   Write a summary of the article reducing it to no more than one third of its original length.

*

4   Read the following article and then write a summary of it, bearing in mind all the instructions and hints you have been given throughout this unit:

A large number of factors influence the way people drink and therefore have a bearing upon whether or not they become alcoholics. These facts can be grouped under two broad headings: firstly, cultural or social factors, and secondly, psychological or internal factors.

It is well known that there are considerable differences between the way alcohol is used in various cultures and that these differences seem to produce considerable variations in alcoholism rates. In Ireland, for example, where heavy drinking is encouraged, drunkenness is tolerated, most drinking takes place outside the family and is not associated with other activities such as eating, there is a particularly high rate of alcoholism. Jews, on the other hand, drink almost exclusively within the family context and do so in a moderate and ritualised way. Alcoholism rates amongst Jews are particularly low. American Mormons, on the other hand, totally prohibit the use of alcohol; yet amongst those who *do* drink, the rate of alcoholism is extremely high. Scotland is generally reckoned to have an alcoholism rate four times that of England and the Highlands and Islands twelve times that of England. Such striking differences cannot be ignored and it seems more than likely that they represent not some biochemical proclivity towards alcoholism in particular racial groups but rather a nexus of socio-cultural attitudes which make certain kinds of drinking behaviour more or less appropriate to most people born into any particular culture.

People working in certain occupations are also known to run a much higher risk of becoming alcoholics. In Table 4 you can see the death rates from cirrhosis of the liver for various occupations.

Table 4 Deaths from cirrhosis in different occupations in England and Wales

	Standard Mortality Ratio
Company Directors	2,200
Publicans	773
Actors and Entertainers	550
Hotel Keepers	450
Armed Forces	350
Medical Practitioners	350
Barmen	200
Commercial Travellers	150
Total male population of England and Wales	100

There are three features which most of these occupations have in common. The first is the availability of free or cheap alcohol. The second is a relative freedom or lack of supervision. The third is a greater than average separation from the stabilising influence of the home. It could of course be argued that potential alcoholics will tend to join these occupational groups in order to ease their problems of supply, but it is surely more likely that the causative relationship works in the opposite direction, particularly when it is borne in mind that the natural history of alcoholism is of a relatively slow progressive condition which usually involves a gradual build-up in quantities being drunk over a number of years. Even although the average age at which alcoholics present themselves for treatment is dropping, it is still true that the commonest age is in the early to mid-40s.

Drinking, as has been suggested already, is a form of habitual behaviour and therefore, like other habits, it has to be learned and reinforced. People learn best by imitation and it seems likely that the drinking behaviour of any individual is influenced most strongly by the drinking behaviour of others close to him – his family and, more particularly, his friends. A degree of uniformity in an important activity like drinking is a strong force for social cohesion. It is hardly coincidental that the majority of people in our society regard total abstinence with suspicion and believe that the fact that abstainers show deviance from the norm in terms of their drinking behaviour is likely to be a sign of inadequacies in other forms of behaviour.

As habitual behaviour becomes what psychologists call functionally autonomous, that is to say when the habit begins to take on a life of its own, we move over from the socio-cultural factors influencing drinking habits to those factors which have to do more with the personality of the individual. There is, as far as we know, no such thing as an alcoholic personality. Nevertheless, people with certain kinds of personalities are obviously more likely to drink excessively than others. This is, however, an extremely difficult area in which to come to any meaningful conclusions, because of the lack of objective scientific criteria. Notions such as 'personality disorders' or 'oral fixations' are likely to prove less than helpful in understanding the aetiology of alcoholism.

Stress is frequently invoked as the major cause of alcoholism. Given the drug effect of alcoholism, its use to relieve stress is clearly of great importance and it may be that many people use alcohol excessively because their life is in some way unbearably stressful. Poverty, overcrowding, family responsibilities, difficulties in marriage, sex or work, loneliness, the state of the nation: anything, in other words, might be the stress. Since the coping mechanism of alcohol is sanctioned by society, the individual could certainly drink in such a way that he becomes in time an alcoholic. What this means is that for many alcoholics there may be no clear-cut distinction between the causes of the condition and the effects of the condition. If alcohol is used as a means of attempting to solve problems, it is likely to exacerbate rather than diminish the difficulties encountered. The more excessive the drinking, the greater the problems are likely to become; and the more excessive still, in turn, becomes the compensating drinking. The alcoholic becomes caught up in a vicious circle where the distinction between cause and effect becomes so blurred as to be almost meaningless. Problems lead to drinking, which leads to

43

greater problems, which lead to more drinking. Or drinking leads to problems, which lead to greater drinking, which leads to more problems. It is the decision of individual therapists to choose the most relevant point of entry into this vicious circle for each alcoholic whom they are called upon to help.

Finally, it is important to note that there is no good evidence, despite exhaustive research, that there are important genetic factors or biochemical abnormalities which would mark out those most at risk. Indeed, on the basis of what we have already seen, it is clear that there is no single cause of alcoholism. A host of different factors combine in different convolutions to produce this elusive but widespread condition. There is, if you like, no such thing as alcoholism. There are many different alcoholisms, each subtly but significantly different from the next, each having a different pattern of causation and perhaps requiring a different kind of treatment.

from 'Understanding Alcoholism and Alcoholism in Scotland'

*

5   At the start of this unit, we emphasised that a passage can only be summarised well if the student understands the intentions of the author and the means by which he is trying to achieve his aim. Review the passages in this unit and discuss the differing intentions of their authors. The following questions will help you to clarify your thoughts.

1   Are any of these passages designed to cause the reader to change his attitudes or views on the topic in question? How does the author attempt to effect this change of view?

2   Which of the pieces is most obviously concerned with conveying information? Does it appeal to the reader's feelings in any way? Does the author categorise the information he gives or comment on it?

3   In which passage does argument figure most prominently? How does the author elaborate his argument?

4   Would you say that any of these authors is most concerned to convey a general feeling for the topic in question, simply to share his knowledge and understanding? Does this type of writing present any particular problems for the summariser?

5   Which passage did you have most difficulty in summarising? Discuss the various difficulties you faced and how you coped with them.

3　Diaries and letters

Diaries

There are two types of diary commonly in use these days: the appointments diary and the private journal. Generally speaking, in the former we make a note of events and engagements before they take place, in an effort to ensure that we do not overlook them. In the latter, we record our impressions of people, places and experiences – as it were – after the event; to remind ourselves in time to come of things which have interested, excited or in some way affected us. It is with this second category that we are here concerned.

Journals are essentially personal documents, seldom – if ever – intended by their authors for general circulation. They are vehicles for our most private thoughts, opinions and feelings. As such, they are bound to differ from each other in their outlook, content and manner in a similar degree to that in which we as individuals differ from each other in our reactions to the experiences of every day. In other words, a diary is as distinct from others of its kind as the individual who compiles it is from others of his. That does not mean to say that one is better or less good than another. Merely that it reveals a different personality, a different way of looking at and recording things.

Here is an excerpt from the journal the writer Katherine Mansfield kept during 1922; when you have read it, consider the questions which follow it:

October 14. I have been thinking this morning until it seems it may get things straightened out if I try to write . . . where I am.

Ever since I came to Paris I have been as ill as ever. In fact, yesterday I thought I was dying. It is not imagination. My heart is so exhausted and so tied up that I can only walk to the taxi and back. I get up at midi and go to bed at 5.30. I try to 'work' by fits and starts, but the time has gone by. I cannot work. Ever since April I have done practically nothing. But why? Because, although Manoukhin's treatment improved my blood and made me look well and did have a good effect on my lungs, it made my heart not one scrap better, and I only won that improvement by living the life of a corpse in the Victoria Palace Hotel.

My spirit is nearly dead. My spring of life is so starved that it's just not dry. Nearly all my improved health is pretence — acting. What does it amount to? Can I walk? Only creep. Can I do anything with my hands or body? Nothing at all. I am an absolutely hopeless invalid. What is my life? It is the existence of a parasite. And five years have passed now, and I am in straiter bonds than ever.

Ah, I feel a little calmer already to be writing. Thank God for writing! I am so terrified of what I am going to do. All the voices out of the 'Past' say 'Don't do it'. Bogey says 'M. is a scientist. He does his part. It's up to you to do yours.' But that is no good at all. I can no more cure my psyche than my body. Less it seems to me. Isn't Bogey himself, perfectly fresh and well, utterly depressed by boils on his neck? Think of five years' imprisonment. Someone has got to help me to get out. If that is a confession of weakness — it is. But it's only lack of imagination that calls it so. And who is going to help me? Remember Switzerland: 'I am helpless.' Of course, he is. One prisoner cannot help another. Do I believe in medicine alone? No, never. In science alone? No, never. It seems to me childish and ridiculous to suppose one can be cured like a cow *if one is not a cow*. And here, all these years, I have been looking for someone who agreed with me. I have heard of Gurdjieff who seems not only to agree but to know infinitely more about it. Why hesitate?

Fear. Fear of what? Doesn't it come down to fear of losing Bogey? I believe it does. But, good Heavens! Face things. What have you of him now? What is your relationship? He talks to you — sometimes — and then goes off. He thinks of you tenderly. He dreams of a life with you *some day* when the miracle has happened. You are important to him as a dream. Not as a living reality. For you are not one. What do you share? Almost nothing. Yet there is a deep, sweet, tender flooding of feeling in my heart which is love for him and longing for him. But what is the good of it as things stand? Life together, with me ill, is simply torture with happy moments. But it's not life. I have tried through my illness

48

(with one or two disastrous exceptions) to prevent him facing wholly what was happening. I ought to have tried to get him to face them. But I couldn't. The result is that he doesn't know me. He only knows Wig-who-is-going-to-be-better-some-day. No. You do know that Bogey and you are only a kind of dream of what might be. And that might-be never never can be true unless you are well. And you won't get well by 'imagining' or 'waiting' or trying to bring off that miracle yourself.

Therefore if the Grand Lama of Thibet promised to help you — how can you hesitate? Risk! Risk anything! Care no more for the opinions of others, for those voices. Do the hardest thing on earth for you. Act for yourself. Face the truth.

from 'The Journal of Katherine Mansfield'

1 What special function of journal-writing is reflected in the opening words of this extract and in Katherine Mansfield's assertion that she feels 'a little calmer already' now that she is writing? How does the mood of the journal change in the course of the extract?

2 One of the special qualities of a diary or journal is its immediacy, the sense of events occurring, of thoughts being born and developed at the very instant of writing. What evidence is there of such immediacy in this passage?

3 Are there any obscurities here, any remarks or references which seem to require further explanation? How do you account for their presence?

4 How closely do we come, by reading these words, to an intimate understanding of Katherine Mansfield's feelings about her life and health? Is there anything here in tone or argument which rings untrue or insincere? Does it help us to know that she tore the pages on which this extract was written from her journal with the intention of sending them to her husband, but that — in the end — she never did so? In what way might she have written differently if she had known that it was to be published for complete strangers to read?

Our second example of diary writing is of a markedly different character. It comes from the journal kept for many years by Francis Kilvert, who spent a good deal of his life as a clergyman in rural Wales. He once reflected on the reasons for his keeping his diary in the following terms:

Why do I keep this voluminous journal? I can hardly tell. Partly because life appears to me such a curious and wonderful thing that it almost seems a pity that even such a humble and uneventful life as mine should pass altogether away without some such record as this, and partly too because I think the record may amuse and interest some who come after me.

Here he is now on Saturday, 26 February, 1870:

My Father's Birthday. Wrote to him and sent him the *Illustrated London Almanac*. A lovely warm morning so I set off to walk over the hills to Colva, taking my luncheon in my pocket, half a dozen biscuits, two apples and a small flask of wine. Took also a pocket book and opera glasses . . . Called at Tymawr and promised Mrs Davies a pair of blankets as she has none. The baby very ill. Went on up the Green Lane. Very hot walking. At the Green Lane Cottage found Mrs Jones and a daughter at home sewing. Mrs Jones remembered me. Price Price sitting half hidden in the chimney corner but alas there was no Abiasula as the last time I was there. Price Price something like his sister Abiasula. A sturdy boy with a round rosy good-humoured face and big black eyes, volunteered to guide me to Colva Church. So he came out of his chimney corner in the ingle nook and we started at once, accompanied by a grey and black sheep-dog puppy. We were out on the open mountain at once. There was the brown withered heather, the elastic turf, the long green ride stretching over the hill like a green ribbon between the dark heather. There was a free fresh fragrant air of the hills, but, oh, for the gipsy lassie with her wild dark eyes under her black hood. We passed 'The Fforest' but she was not to be seen. Price Price recognised and named the Black Mountain, but did not know the Fan of Brecon. As we went down the Fuallt a grouse cock uttered his squirling crow and flew over the crest of the hill. I had never heard a grouse crow before. 'What's that bird crying?' I said to the boy. 'A grouse', he said, adding, 'There he goes over the bank. They be real thick hereabout'.

Tried to get across the swift Arrow (swollen by the junction of the Glasnant just above) by climbing along a rail but we failed and had to go up a meadow till we got above the meeting of the waters, when we crossed the Glasnant on a hurdle laid flat over the stream and then we jumped the Arrow. Up the steep breast of the Reallt to Dol Reallt and along the road to the Wern and Bryntwyn from whence a field path leads to Colva Church. Here Price Price left me after showing me across one field. I asked him to have some bread and cheese and beer at the Sun Inn, Colva, but he would not and could scarcely be prevailed on to take sixpence. Tried the echo in the field against the belfrey and west end of the poor humble dear little white-washed church sequestered among its large ancient yews. Richard Meredith told me of this echo. Mrs Phillips, the landlady of the Sun, was much frightened when I asked for her husband, uneasy and nervous lest I should have come to apprehend him for having been in a row or doing something wrong. But when I said I wanted the words of an old song, she was greatly relieved and said at once 'Oh I know who you are. You are the gentleman from Clyro.' I laughed and she began to smile. Mrs Phillips took me into the parlour where I sat down, tore a leaf out of my pocket book and wrote with my request that Phillips would send me by post 1. the song about our Saviour, 2. the song about Lazarus, 3. the song about King James and the Tinker. Mrs Phillips brought me a pint of excellent light, bright beer, some hard sweet homebaked bread, and some hard cheese, carrying the bread and cheese in her arms as she ran with it, as I was in a hurry to push on . . . At Gilfach-y-rheol Vaughan sitting on a sofa with a nose fearfully swollen with a carbuncle, but it is better and he hopes to be able to do duty at Bryngwyn, Newchurch and Bettws tomorrow. His son John from Llwyn Gwillim had come over and was sitting with him. They made me stay to tea and I was thirsty but could eat nothing at four o'clock after luncheon at the Sun at Colva so shortly before. John went home before tea. At tea there were Sarah, Emmeline with her Geneva brooch and fair curls and saucy Jinny with her dark eyes. She gave me a kiss at parting. I found Matilda and Willie in the Kitchen, and I met Willie in the village. Went home by Llwyn Gwillim and reached Clyro just in time to dress for dinner at Cae Mawr. But as I was going out I was sent for to baptize Mrs Jones the Jockey's baby opposite and I was only too thankful that it was so near and that I had not to right about face and march back up to the top of Clyro Hill again. The child was said to suffer from convulsions, so I baptized it, but it was probably quite well. The name selected was as far as I could make out Mahalah which Mrs Jones declared to be the name of one of Cain's wives, on the authority of a book she had read called the Life of Abel. She called her elder girl Thirza, which she says was the name of Cain's other wife. Not a happy allusion.

from 'Journal of a Country Curate' by Francis Kilvert

1   Which details give this passage the ring of authenticity and truth? How do they help convey what life in Kilvert's time must have been like?

2   In what essentials are Katherine Mansfield's and Francis Kilvert's diaries alike, and in what essentials are they different? What can we learn from our observation about the nature and range of journals of this sort?

3   How much does Kilvert really reveal about himself in his journal? In what ways does it reflect his personality? Was he justified in describing his journal and his motives for writing as he did in the short passage we have quoted? Is it possible to deduce anything of his character from his writings?

Prepare two parallel journals for yesterday, one in the style of Katherine Mansfield, and the other in that of Francis Kilvert.

Personal letters

Consider the different types of conversation that you are in the habit of pursuing.

1   Suppose that you are spending time with a close friend or a relative that you have not seen for a while. What sort of topics would you be likely to talk about? How would your conversation develop and what thoughts might prompt the introduction of new topics? Would you describe your conversation as orderly, working through a structured range of ideas, or would it be random? Suppose that your friend, always, regularly, without fail, disagrees with you over certain issues (politics or sex, or religion, or the pop-scene), how might you embark on a discussion of one of these topics?

2   Imagine, on the other hand, a conversation with an acquaintance, not an intimate friend, who asks you to tell him about a holiday from which you have recently returned, or about a film you have seen, or who asks for your opinion on some issue affecting school or college life,

politics or sport or what you will. How might such a conversation develop? Is there likely to be as much interruption or random interchange of ideas as in the more intimate conversation?

Develop, in pairs, two improvised conversations assuming, in the first case, that you are close friends who know a great deal about each other and, in the second case, that you are only acquaintances. Decide where the conversation is taking place and what topics you are going to talk about before you begin the improvisation. Then discuss in the whole group what you have learnt about interpersonal communication. In addition to the questions implied above, you might consider how much communication takes place through gestures and manner and how much communication may be implied, merely hinted at, not spelt out at length.

Personal letters, like conversations, will reflect the degree of intimacy which we have established with our correspondents. Their stylistic range will be as varied as our personalities and relationships. There are no rules governing their content and manner of writing other than that they should closely reflect the relationships we have with our correspondents. Very often our letters must be a poor substitute for a face to face meeting; on other occasions, we may be able to communicate thoughts far more coherently in a letter than we would in a conversation with the same person.

Here are two letters written in very different styles. The first is from the poet, Wilfred Owen to his mother, written in the trenches of the First World War less than a month before he was killed. The 'great concerns' to which he refers in the opening sentence are an attack on the Beaurevoir-Fonsomme Line carried out on the 1st October 1918 and succeeding counter attacks. The second is by the novelist D. H. Lawrence. Whilst travelling in Germany in 1928, he describes his feelings about the country to a friend.

1 Not for circulation as a whole.

Dearest of Mothers,

No letter from you today, and no parcel. The great concerns which take my time have prevented me from properly thanking you for the many little blessings of your last parcel. The Munchie I ate over a period of several days & nights; and the fact that it was once eaten under a particularly nasty and accurate bombard-ment — (shells so close that they thoroughly put the wind up a Life Guardsman in the trench with me — so that he shook as the Guards shake on parade) these circumstances, I say, have not taken the good savour from Munchie-munchie.

The New Food served me one night when we lay drenched to the bone, and the awful Cold had begun to paralyse my stomach. I don't like this Food.

On that night both officers & men lay in the mud utterly despondent; but a lance-corporal spread half his blanket (not supposed to be carried) over me, and the warmth came like the rising of the May-day sun. So I was saved from the nearest approach to the excruciation of my First Campaign. That time on the Somme in 1917 was so infinitely worse than this for cold, privation, and fatigue that nothing daunts me now.

The Sergeant, now acting my Coy Sgt Major, was a corporal with me in the first dug-out where the Sentry was blinded, you remember. He remembers it . . .

I still command D Coy and have now four junior officers.

It is delightful to have the Scarborough Drums to fill the Vacant Ranks. Censoring letters today I came across this: 'Do you know that little officer called Owen who was at Scarborough; he is commanding my Company, and he is a *toff* I can tell you. No na-poo. Compree?' Interpreted: 'a fine fellow, no nonsense about him!'

I record this because it is more pleasing than military medals with many bars.

Returning to the unpacking of my parcels: cigarettes: arrived just in time: sweets & (good) chocolate always welcome.

You see I live between the extremes of gross materialism — feeding savagely & sleeping doggishly — and of high spirituality — suffering & sacrificing.

Wilfred.

(1928)

2 We are going back to Paris tomorrow, so this is the last moment to write a letter from Germany. Only from the fringe of Germany, too.

It is a miserable journey from Paris to Nancy, through that Marne country, where the country still seems to have had the soul blasted out of it, though the dreary fields are ploughed and level, and the pale wire trees stand up. But it is all void and null. And in the villages, the smashed houses in the street rows, like rotten teeth between good teeth.

You come to Strasbourg, and the people still talk Alsatian German, as ever, in spite of French shop-signs. The place feels dead. And full of cottage goods, white goods, from Mulhausen, from the factories that once were German. Such cheap white cotton goods, in a glut.

The cathedral front rearing up high and flat and fanciful, a sort of darkness in the dark, with round rose windows and long, long prisons of stone. Queer that men should have ever wanted to put stone upon faithful stone to such a height without having it fall down. The gothic! I was always glad when my card-castle fell. But these goths and alemans seemed to have a craze for peaky heights.

The Rhine is still the Rhine, the great divider. You feel it as you cross. The flat, frozen, watery places. Then the cold and curving river. Then the other side, seeming so cold, so empty, so frozen, so foresaken. The train stands and steams fiercely. Then it draws through the flat Rhine plain, past frozen pools of flood-water, and frozen fields, in the emptiness of this bit of occupied territory.

Immediately you are over the Rhine, the spirit of place has changed. There is no more attempt at the bluff of geniality. The marshy places are frozen. The fields are vacant. There seems nobody in the world.

It is as if the life had retreated eastwards. As if the Germanic life were slowly ebbing away from contact with western Europe, ebbing to the deserts of the east. And there stand the heavy, ponderous round hills of the Black Forest, black with an inky blackness of Germanic trees, and patched with a whiteness of snow. They are like a series of huge, involved black mounds, obstructing the vision eastwards. You look at them from the Rhine plain, and know that you stand on an actual border, up against something.

The moment you are in Germany, you know. It feels empty, and, somehow, menacing. So must the Roman soldiers have watched those black, massive round hills: with a certain fear, and with the knowledge that they were at their own limit. A fear of the invisible natives. A fear of the invisible life lurking among the woods. A fear of their own opposite.

So it is with the French: this almost mystic fear. But one should not insult even one's fears.

Germany, this bit of Germany, is very different from what it was two and a half years ago, when I was here. Then it was still open to Europe. Then it still looked to western Europe for a reunion, for a sort of reconciliation. Now that is over. The inevitable, mysterious barrier has fallen again, and the great leaning of the Germanic spirit is once more eastwards, towards Russia, towards Tartary. The strange vortex of Tartary has become the positive centre again, the positivity of western Europe is broken. The positivity of our civilisation has broken. The influences that come, come invisibly out of Tartary. So that all Germany reads *Men, Beasts and Gods* with a kind of fascination. Returning again to the fascination of the destructive East, that produced Attila.

So it is at night. Baden-Baden is a little quiet place, all its guests gone. No more Turgenevs or Dostoevskys or Grand Dukes or King Edwards coming to drink the waters. All the outward effect of a worldfamous watering-place. But empty now, a mere Black Forest village with the wagon-loads of timber going through, to the French.

The Rentenmark, the new gold Mark of Germany, is abominably dear. Prices are high in England, but English money buys less in Baden than it buys in London, by a long chalk. And there is no work — consequently no money. Nobody buys anything, except absolute necessities. The shopkeepers are in despair. And there is less and less work.

Everybody gives up the telephone — can't afford it. The tramcars don't run, except about three times a day to the station. Up to the Annaberg, the suburb, the lines are rusty, no trams ever go. The people can't afford the ten pfennigs for the fare. Ten pfennigs is an important sum now: one penny. It is really a hundred Milliards of Marks.

Money becomes insane, and people with it.

At night the place is almost dark, economising light. Economy, economy, economy — that, too, becomes an insanity. Luckily the government keeps bread fairly cheap.

But at night you feel strange things stirring in the darkness, strange feelings stirring out of this still unconquered Black Forest.

You stiffen your backbone and you listen to the night. There is a
sense of danger. It is not the people. They don't seem dangerous.
Out of the very air comes a sense of danger, a queer, *bristling*
feeling of uncanny danger. . . . .

    D. H. Lawrence

1   Which of these two letters would you be most pleased to receive
and why? Their styles contrast very clearly. Which of them would you
be most likely to write?

2   Which details in Wilfred Owen's letter show that it is part of a
very close relationship between the writer and his mother? Is there
anything in the letter which gives us any insight into the character of
Susan Owen?

3   Lawrence does not refer directly to any aspect of his
correspondent's life or personality. Does this mean that we must regard
his writing here as more of a literary exercise, a sort of essay, than a
successful letter?

4   Discuss the structure and organisation of these two letters. How
does Lawrence proceed so as to draw his reader into an appreciation of
his experience and thought about Germany? What evidence is there for
saying that Owen writes from spontaneous impulse rather than from a
desire to present a controlled and orderly account of his experiences?

Bearing in mind the different styles of the letters you have examined,
write a couple of letters of your own. There is no reason why they
should not be written to real people and posted to them. But even if they
are to remain as writing exercises, keep in mind your possible
correspondents and try to achieve a contrast between the more intimate,
spontaneous style and the more detached and controlled letter.

Business letters

Whereas in a personal letter the writer's intention may be to recreate the
atmosphere of a scene or an event, to describe his innermost feelings or
to capture a mood, the purpose of a business letter is to convey
information. Business letters are, therefore, written in a more direct,
impersonal style. The writer adopts a formal tone in keeping with the
purpose of his letter. A formal layout is also used. The name and address
of the person to whom the letter is being sent is included, as well as the
address of the writer and the date. If a copy of the letter is kept, both the

writer and the person to whom it is sent thus have a complete record of their dealings with one another, to which they can refer in the future, if necessary.

It is important when you are writing business letters not only to adopt the appropriate tone, but also to bear in mind the purpose of the letter and to stick to the point. A good business letter is clear and concise and does not include any distracting anecdotes or unnecessary, irrelevant details. Here is an example of such a letter:

Sir Thomas Copcutt School,
Observatory Road,
Newtown.

Mr R. Jenkins,
15 Manor Court,
Eastern Road,
Newtown.

18th September 1978

Dear Mr Jenkins,

I am writing on behalf of the sixth form common room committee of Sir Thomas Copcutt School. We are organising a disco on Friday, November 14th in the school hall. The disco will start at 8.00 p.m. and finish at 11.30 p.m. We would like to hire the Sounds Alive disco, which you run, for that evening.

I am enclosing a stamped addressed envelope and would be grateful if you could let me know as soon as possible if you are available. Please could you also let me know what the hire charge will be.

Yours sincerely,
Clare Ashton
(Secretary, Sixth Form
Common Room Committee)

1   Write to a music shop, or to a book-shop, asking them to order for you a record or a book, which you have had difficulty in obtaining.

2   Write to a camp site, holiday caravan park or to a boarding house, to book a short holiday for yourself and some friends.

3   Study the advertisements for jobs in a newspaper and write a letter of application for one of them.

4   Look at the entertainments advertised in one of the national newspapers. Write a letter to the box office manager of a theatre to book tickets for a concert or a play.

5   An article, which you bought while on holiday, has broken. It is

still under guarantee. Write either to the shop where you bought it, or to the manufacturers, explaining what has happened and asking them to do something about it.

6   You have seen a newspaper advertisement with a box number advertising an item which interests you, for example a second-hand motor-bike or audio-system. Write a letter asking for further details.

7   You left an article on a bus or in a train. Write a letter to enquire whether it has been found.

8   You own a motor-scooter and have been involved in an accident. Write a letter to your insurance company, explaining exactly what happened.

Open letters

Open letters are letters written to newspapers or magazines. Sometimes the writer is concerned merely to state a fact, in order to point out an error that the newspaper or magazine made in one of its reports or articles. More often, the writer's purpose is to develop an argument in response to an article or report in a previous edition or to put forward a point of view on an issue that the writer considers of such significance that it should be brought to the attention of the public in either a national or a local newspaper. The most important point to remember when writing an open letter is to structure your argument carefully and not to allow your emotions to cloud your argument. People frequently write to newspapers because they are incensed about something. Their writing can become so emotive that they include irrelevant points, which weaken the strength of their argument, and can give the reader the impression that their viewpoint is such a biased one that it is not worthy of serious consideration.

Study some letters in some recent newspapers. Can you find any in which the writer has either overstated his case or weakened his argument, by going off at a tangent rather than developing the main point?

The following editorial appeared in the *Times Educational Supplement* on 19 May 1978. Read it and then write an open letter in reaction to it, stating your views on whether or not the government should force everyone to adopt metric measurements.

Cold feet on metrication

What a ludicrous mess the Government and those vote-conscious back-benchers have got into by their shilly-shallying over the final stages of metrication. It is tiresome enough for adults who have to calculate measurements of anything from a carpet to a cupboard in metric and imperial because some shops are going it alone while others are dragging their feet until they are forced into conversion.

What is really serious is that everyone seems to have overlooked the effect it is going to have on our school-leavers. During the past ten years the schools have switched to teaching the metric system, and it has been adopted by the exam boards as a matter of policy to fit in with the announced Government timetable. Yet children will now continue to leave school for a world, and more important an industry, which is in many places hanging on to measurements which are no longer taught in many schools.

What on earth is the point of industrialists and politicians sounding off about bringing school and industry closer together, and calling for better standards of numeracy to do the trick, when they apparently lack the will to achieve uniformity on something so basic as weights and measures?

from 'The Times Educational Supplement', 19 May 1978

While the majority of open letters are written in response to a statement previously made or reported in the newspaper or magazine, others, such as the one printed below, are written in order to raise a particular issue and focus public attention on it. Notice how the writer of this letter presents her argument clearly and concisely, and does not wander from the point.

Responsibility and the Pill

SIR – In spite of argument to the contrary, let us please try unemotively to observe one fact. The 'pill' as a contraceptive is believed to be absolutely effective. It therefore follows that those women who regularly and responsibly take their pill, no matter how irregular or irresponsible their sex-lives may be, do not contribute to illegitimacy rates nor to abortion rates. Promiscuity without contraception is what does so.

Personally I believe that if an unmarried sixteen-year-old is promiscuous, it is better and less expensive for society for her to take the pill than to have an abortion on the National Health Service, or an illegitimate baby on the Department of Health and

Social Security; it is also less destructive for her and for her putative child.

Minnow Chris Dalglish,
Clifton, Bristol.

from 'The Daily Telegraph', 22 April 1978

1 Write a letter in response to the above letter or a letter on an issue which you feel should be aired in the columns of a national newspaper.

2 Write a letter to your local newspaper on a local issue about which you have strong feelings.

Here are a number of letters which appeared in response to the article *The nasty sound of youth* which was printed in *The Sunday Telegraph* on 9 April 1978 and which is included in the unit of Journalism (See p. 107). Read the article and then the letters.

The nasty sound of youth

Peregrine Worsthorne's article about modern youth was very timely. Adults today do not make rules, which youngsters need and like to make clear when authority is being offended (ask any pupils in schools that believe rules are unfashionable); or, if they do not make rules, they cannot be bothered to enforce them, because they lack either the will or the courage to be unpopular with their children, whom they feel they must humour, if only for the quiet life.

The longer these irresponsible 'turn-the-other-way' and 'don't-get-involved' attitudes continue, the worse the situation — and the backlash — will be.

Geoffrey H. Peake, Pilton, Devon.

Even public libraries, which should be an oasis of quietude, have been corrupted by those who wish to destroy the civilised environment. Our own library is frequently resorted to by parents with uncontrollable toddlers, who run round and round the shelves, sometimes removing books, or who set up an unchecked howling for no apparent reason, and are neither reproved nor removed.

Last week I mentioned to two seventeen-year-old boys who

were trying to dribble a football round the shelves without being seen by a librarian, that this was not the place for football. One of them said that he was depressed. I told him that I would not respond to such an obvious attempt to enlist my sympathy as in his attempt thus to wear 'his heart on his sleeve'. I forebear to give you details of the local vandals. They are just too depressing.

E. Turnbull, Gosforth, Northumberland.

I read with much interest the article by Peregrine Worsthorne 'The nasty sound of youth'. The ever-increasing crime-rate begins among school children and, as far as the Borough of Lewisham is concerned, it would appear that no-one in authority cares very much. Children are turned out into the streets from home and school to destroy and annoy. In my own road we have counted as many as sixty children at one time, terrorising the neighbourhood on skateboards and rollerskates, by stone-throwing and general hooliganism. This used to be a quiet residential area.

(Mrs) Doreen M. Williams, Secretary, Borough of Lewisham Chamber of Commerce and Trade, London, S.E. 13.
from 'The Sunday Telegraph', 16 April 1978

Lack of influence by parents

I was appalled at reading the replies to Peregrine Worsthorne's 'The nasty sound of youth'. I, myself, am a sixteen-year-old schoolgirl, and having travelled around the country (my father's occupation necessitating it) I have had a wide experience of a fair cross-section of schools.

It was with dismay, then, that I read the opinions of two supposedly sensible adults. I feel they have missed the point of the article — children are brought up and taught their social code, and by whom? Adults. What Peregrine Worsthorne was saying was that it is the parents who are at fault, and not so much the children. It seems to me that the older generation of today are generally acting like Dickensian characters, forgetting that they themselves were once young.

I could not help agreeing with Geoffrey H. Peake's opinion that too many adults would rather 'give in' to their children than be unpopular with them, which to my mind, only causes more resentment. The number of friends I have whom I enviously watch going everywhere and doing everything because their parents 'don't mind' (or to be more precise 'don't care') proves this point. But who is the better off really?

I think adults are being irresponsible and we do need a moral code. If you only realised that hooliganism is a direct plea for a stable set of rules, then perhaps you would see where the problem lies.

W. J. Malpass, Biggin Hill, Kent.
from 'The Sunday Telegraph', 23 April 1978

1 In which of the letters do you think the argument is most effectively presented? Explain why.

2 Write your own letter in response to the article and to these letters.

4   The essay

Write an essay on *The Results of the Treaty of Utrecht.* . . . on *Your Hobbies.* . . . on *Visiting Relations.* . . . on *Nuclear Disarmament.* . . . on *The Pleasures of Travel.* . . . on *The Uses of Poetry.* . . . on *The Effects of Glaciation on Limestone Areas.* . . . and on a thousand and one other topics covering all subjects of study and many areas of personal experience. The request for an essay will have echoed throughout your school career and the demands implied in each of these requests will have been different, for 'the essay' is a remarkably flexible literary form capable of adaptation to a range of different purposes.

Discuss together the different sorts of essay that you have been required to write. You might proceed by choosing a topic on which you have recently written as part of your normal academic studies and considering the way you set about writing the essay. Contrast that procedure with the way you would write an essay on a topic like *The Pleasures of Travel.* What preparatory thinking would be appropriate for each of these topics before you started writing? How would you organise your material within each of these essays? Would the problems you encountered in writing the essays be the same?

It is not so easy to say exactly what an essay is even when we consider those essays which have become a part of our literary tradition. For the concept depends largely on the literary conventions of any age in which a particular essayist happens to write. The earliest English essayists, such as Francis Bacon, who was writing in Elizabethan and Jacobean times, were primarily inspired by a high moral purpose. Conscious of his own learning and wisdom, Bacon wished to present his own philosophy of life in his essays so that others might benefit. Although his essays are eminently readable, his purpose is less to entertain than to improve the life of his readers.

In the last part of the seventeenth century and the early part of the eighteenth, a different type of essay emerged. Richard Steele and Joseph Addison began writing essays which were published in periodicals such as *The Tatler* or *Spectator.* Subscribers to these periodicals wanted to be interested and amused rather than preached at and so essayists chose homely or topical themes and wrote in a familiar, personal style. It is this sort of essay that Dr Johnson defined in his *Dictionary* (1755) as 'a loose sally of the mind: an irregular, undigested piece: not a regular and orderly composition.' The definition suggested spontaneity and a personal quality in the writing of the essay. The author chose any topic and would develop his subject by including anecdotes and personal experience of all sorts and by carefully defining the exact quality of his feelings about the topic. Thoughts would, therefore, arise from the author's own real or fictionalised memories, in contrast with earlier essayists who started with an abstract topic and included examples only by way of illustration. A. C. Benson summed up this particular type of essay when he described it, in *The Art of the Essayist*, as, 'personal sensation, personal impression, evoked by something strange or beautiful or curious or interesting or amusing'.

As you read through the modern essays included in this chapter, that is, those by Orwell, Lynd and Huxley, consider how these more recent writers have adapted the essay form to suit their own needs.

The essay of ideas

Essays which present arguments fall into two broad categories: those which are designed primarily to open up a subject for the reader's further consideration, and those in which the writer's purpose is to persuade the reader of the rightness of a particular point of view. In the first of the essays in this section Francis Bacon presents a range of arguments on a topic in order to stimulate the reader to further thought, while in the second, George Orwell's aim is to develop his argument so as to influence his readers to share his opinions. In the third, Robert Lynd sets out to entertain his readers and at the same time to make a serious point.

Of marriage and single life

He that hath wife and children hath given hostages to fortune; for they are impediments to great enterprises, either of virtue or mischief. Certainly, the best works, and of greatest merit for the public, have proceeded from the unmarried or childless men, which both in affection and means have married and endowed the public. Yet it were great reason that those that have children should have greatest care of future times; unto which they know they must transmit their dearest pledges. Some there are, who though they lead a single life, yet their thoughts do end with themselves, and account future times impertinences. Nay, there are some other that account wife and children but as bills of charges. Nay more, there are some foolish rich covetous men that take a pride in having no children, because they may be thought so much the richer. For perhaps they have heard some talk, 'Such an one is a great rich man', and another except to it, 'Yea, but he hath a great charge of children'; as if it were an abatement to his riches. But the most ordinary cause of a single life is liberty; especially in certain selfpleasing and humorous minds, which are so sensible of every restraint, as they will go near to think their girdles and garters to be bonds and shackles. Unmarried men are best friends, best masters, best servants; but not always best subjects; for they are light to run away; and almost all fugitives are of that condition. A single life doth well with churchmen; for charity will hardly water the ground where it must first fill a pool. It is indifferent for judges and magistrates; for if they be facile and corrupt, you shall have a servant five times worse than a wife. For soldiers, I find the generals commonly in their hortatives put men in mind of their wives and children; and I think the despising of marriage amongst the Turks maketh the vulgar soldier more base. Certainly wife and children are a kind of discipline of humanity; and single men, though they be many times more charitable, because their means are less exhaust, yet, on the other side, they are more cruel and hard-hearted (good to make severe inquisitors), because their tenderness is not so oft called upon. Grave natures, led by custom, and therefore constant, are commonly loving husbands; as was said of Ulysses, 'Vetulam suam proetulit immortalitati'. Chaste women are often proud and froward, as presuming upon the merit of their chastity. It is one of the best bonds both of chastity and obedience in the wife, if she think her husband wise; which she will never do if she find him jealous. Wives are young men's mistresses; companions for middle age; and old men's nurses. So as a man may have a quarrel to marry when he will. But yet he was reputed one of the wise men, that made answer to the question, when a man should marry? 'A young man not yet, an elder man not at all.' It is often seen that bad husbands have very good wives; whether it be that it raises the price of their husband's kindness when it comes; or that the wives take a pride in their patience. But this never fails, if the bad husbands were of their own choosing, against their friends' consent; for then they will be sure to make good their own folly.

Francis Bacon

1 Study the essay carefully to decide whether Bacon is more in favour of marriage or of single life. List the statements that he makes in favour of marriage. What arguments does he use to support these statements? List the statements that he makes in favour of single life. What arguments does he present to support these statements?

Bacon was writing at the beginning of the seventeenth century. Discuss his views. Do you agree or disagree violently with any of them? Why?

What other advantages or disadvantages of marriage or single life are there besides those that Bacon mentions? Organise a debate on a motion either 'This house believes that the advantages of marriage outweigh its disadvantages', or 'This house prefers to remain single'.

2 To write essays in Bacon's style is far from easy, for he had the ability, which few of us possess, to condense his thoughts and to express complex ideas simply and concisely. Though we may not be able to reproduce his style, we can, however, benefit from adopting his approach to a subject, for it enables us to see a topic from a variety of angles and to focus on aspects of it that we might otherwise have failed to consider. Using an approach similar to Bacon's consider the question of disarmament. Think about it from every conceivable angle – economic, political, moral, military, and write down the different statements that might be made about disarmament by a wide range of people from a pacifist to an owner of a munitions factory. Discuss your list of statements together, then decide upon a motion and organise a debate on the theme of disarmament.

3 Use the procedure outlined above to collect your thoughts on either i) the advantages and disadvantages of living in the city rather than the country, or ii) the reasons for, and arguments against, paying people who do skilled, dangerous or responsible jobs more money than workers doing unskilled, less dangerous or less responsible jobs. Either write an essay on 'Living in the city and in the country' or on 'Money and Work', or organise a debate on a motion connected with one of these topics.

The sporting spirit

Now that the brief visit of the Dynamo football team* has come to an end, it is possible to say publicly what many thinking people were saying privately before the Dynamos ever arrived. That is, that sport is an unfailing cause of ill-will, and that if such a visit as this had any effect at all on Anglo-Soviet relations, it could only be to make them slightly worse than before.

Even the newspapers have been unable to conceal the fact that at least two of the four matches played led to much bad feeling. At the Arsenal match, I am told by someone who was there, a British and a Russian player came to blows and the crowd booed the referee. The Glasgow match, someone else informs me, was simply a free-for-all from the start. And then there was the controversy, typical of our nationalistic age, about the composition of the Arsenal team. Was it really an all-England team, as claimed by the Russians, or merely a league team, as claimed by the British? And did the Dynamos end their tour abruptly in order to avoid playing an all-England team? As usual, everyone answers these questions according to his political predilections. No doubt the controversy will continue to echo for years in the footnotes of history books. Meanwhile the result of the Dynamo's tour, in so far as it has had any result, will have been to create fresh animosity on both sides.

And how could it be otherwise? I am always amazed when I hear people saying that sport creates goodwill between the nations, and that if only the common peoples of the world could meet one another at football or cricket, they would have no inclination to meet on the battlefield. Even if one didn't know from concrete examples (the 1936 Olympic Games, for instance) that international sporting contests lead to orgies of hatred, one could deduce it from general principles.

Nearly all the sports practised nowadays are competitive. You play to win, and the game has little meaning unless you do your utmost to win. On the village green, where you pick up sides and no feeling of local patriotism is involved, it is possible to play simply for the fun and exercise: but as soon as the question of

---

* The Moscow Dynamos, a Russian football team, toured Britain in the autumn of 1945 playing against leading clubs.

prestige arises, as soon as you feel that you and some larger unit will be disgraced if you lose, the most savage combative instincts are aroused. Anyone who has played even in a school football match knows this. At the international level sport is frankly mimic warfare. But the significant thing is not the behaviour of the players but the attitude of the spectators: and, behind the spectators, of the nations who work themselves into furies over these absurd contests, and seriously believe – at any rate for short periods – that running, jumping and kicking a ball are tests of national virtue.

Even a leisurely game like cricket, demanding grace rather than strength, can cause much ill-will, as we saw in the controversy over body-line bowling and over the rough tactics of the Australian team that visited England in 1921. Football, a game in which everyone gets hurt and every nation has its own style of play which seems unfair to foreigners, is far worse. Worst of all is boxing. One of the most horrible sights in the world is a fight between white and coloured boxers before a mixed audience. But a boxing audience is always disgusting, and the behaviour of the women, in particular, is such that the Army, I believe, does not allow them to attend its contests. At any rate, two or three years ago, when Home Guards and regular troops were holding a boxing tournament, I was placed on guard at the door of the hall, with orders to keep women out.

In England, the obsession with sport is bad enough, but even fiercer passions are aroused in young countries where game-playing and nationalism are both recent developments. In countries like India or Burma, it is necessary at football matches to have strong cordons of police to keep the crowd from invading the field. In Burma, I have seen the supporters of one side break through the police and disable the goalkeeper of the opposing side at a critical moment. The first big football match that was played in Spain about fifteen years ago, led to an uncontrollable riot. As soon as strong feelings of rivalry are aroused, the notion of playing the game according to the rules always vanishes. People want to see one side on top and the other side humiliated and they forget that victory gained through cheating or through the intervention of the crowd is meaningless. Even when the spectators don't intervene physically they try to influence the game by cheering their own side and 'rattling' opposing players with boos and insults. Serious sport has nothing to do with fair play. It is bound up with hatred, jealousy, boastfulness, disregard of all rules and sadistic pleasure in witnessing violence: in other words it is war minus the shooting.

Instead of blah-blahing about the clean, healthy rivalry of the football field and the great part played by the Olympic Games in bringing the nations together, it is more useful to inquire how and why this modern cult of sport arose. Most of the games we now play are of ancient origin, but sport does not seem to have been taken very seriously between Roman times and the nineteenth century. Even in the English public schools the games cult did not start till the latter part of the last century. Dr Arnold, generally regarded as the founder of the modern public school, looked on games as simply a waste of time. Then, chiefly in England and the United States, games were built up into a heavily-financed activity, capable of attracting vast crowds and arousing savage passions, and the infection spread from country to country. It is the most violently combative sports, football and boxing, that have spread the widest. There cannot be much doubt that the whole thing is bound up with the rise of nationalism — that is, with the lunatic modern habit of identifying oneself with large power units and seeing everything in terms of competitive prestige. Also, organised games are more likely to flourish in urban communities where the average human being lives a sedentary or at least a confined life, and does not get much opportunity for creative labour. In a rustic community a boy or young man works off a good deal of his surplus energy by walking, swimming, snowball-ing, climbing trees, riding horses, and by various sports involving cruelty to animals, such as fishing, cock-fighting and ferreting for rats. In a big town one must indulge in group activities if one wants an outlet for one's physical strength or for one's sadistic impulses. Games are taken seriously in London and New York, and they were taken seriously in Rome and Byzantium: in the Middle Ages they were played, and probably played with much physical brutality, but they were not mixed up with politics nor a cause of group hatreds.

If you wanted to add to the vast fund of ill-will existing in the world at this moment, you could hardly do it better than by a series of football matches between Jews and Arabs, Germans and Czechs, Indians and British, Russians and Poles, and Italians and Yugoslavs, each match to be watched by a mixed audience of 100 000 spectators. I do not, of course, suggest that sport is one of the main causes of international rivalry; big-scale sport is itself, I think, merely another effect of the causes that have produced nationalism. Still, you do make things worse by sending forth a team of eleven men, labelled as national champions, to do battle against some rival team, and allowing it to be felt on all sides that whichever nation is defeated will 'lose face'.

I hope, therefore, that we shan't follow up the visit of the Dynamos by sending a British team to the USSR. If we must do so, then let us send a second-rate team which is sure to be beaten and cannot be claimed to represent Britain as a whole. There are quite enough real causes of trouble already, and we need not add to them by encouraging young men to kick each other on the shins amid the roars of infuriated spectators.

George Orwell

1   Summarise in a single sentence the point of view that Orwell is expressing in this essay.

2   Consider the title of the essay. Is it a good title? Why? Suggest a number of possible alternatives.

3   Study the structure of the essay. Look closely at each of the nine paragraphs, then draw a flow diagram to show how the ideas from one paragraph lead into the next and how Orwell develops his argument. Notice how he uses a particular example to enable him to make a general point and then how he rounds off his argument by referring back to the particular example with which he began.

4   Orwell's essay is very emotive. Discuss the language that he uses. Find examples of his use of language that reveal how strongly he feels about this issue.

5   This essay was written in 1945. Talk about how international sport has developed since then. Discuss Orwell's views in the light of these developments. Do you agree or disagree with his views. Why?

6   Write an essay **either** (i) attacking or defending Orwell's point of view;

or (ii) expressing the view that the way British people keep and treat pets is ridiculous;

or (iii) arguing for the introduction of one year's national community or military service for everyone before they reach the age of 21.

The militant rambler

An idealist has written a letter to a morning paper, urging an intensification of the propaganda against litter on the eve of Bank Holidays. He also appeals to the BBC to announce, as soon as a Bank Holiday is over, the names of the various places where paper and rubbish have been left by holiday-makers. 'This,' he believes, 'would probably "touch" the consciences of the guilty.'

This, I think, is one of the most attractive proposals that have been made in the course of the anti-litter campaign. It is attractive not because of the results it may be expected to produce, but because of the faith in human nature which it demonstrates. I would give a great deal to be able to believe that the ordinary litter-thrower is a man with a conscience so sensitive that he would blench on hearing it announced from his loud-speaker that the sandwich-wrapping which he had carelessly thrown away in a field near Neasden had been discovered. But I cannot believe it. Besides, there would be such a cornucopia of litter strewn in the most thickly frequented beautyspots that the individual litter-thrower would feel that his own sin was scarcely noticeable in the composite sin of the multitude. Suppose, for example, that a man threw away the core of an apple on Box Hill on a Bank Holiday. Would he turn pale with a sense of guilt discovered when the BBC announcer made it known the next day that a thousand and fifty-nine pieces of newspaper, four hundred and eighty-three squares of brown paper, six thousand seven hundred and five scraps of orange peel, nine empty Mobil oil tins, an old boot, twelve beer bottles, twelve hundred and two chocolate wrappings, eighty-one chicken bones, three burst balloons, one apple-core, and seven hundred and nineteen empty cigarette packets were reported to have been discovered on and under Box Hill after the holiday? Would he not feel that his apple core was an inconspicuous trifle amid so monstrous a mass of rubbish? His indignation, it seems to me, would be directed against the other people who had destroyed the amenities of Box Hill with their mountains of litter, not against himself.

At the same time, if it were possible, it would be an excellent thing, after every Bank Holiday, to publish the statistics of litter-throwing and of its geographical distribution. The imagination of the public might be struck if it were announced that the paper and rubbish thrown away in Sussex alone in a single day would, if brought into the same place, form a heap two and a half times as large as Chanctonbury Hill. Unfortunately, if the BBC attempted to publish a complete account of all the litter thrown away by the public on a Bank Holiday, another Bank Holiday would have come round long before the catalogue of the rubbish was complete. And how monotonous it would become. 'Under a chestnut-tree near Friday Street, a petrol tin was left behind by a motorist on Easter Sunday.' 'A sardine tin containing oil and the mutilated tail of a sardine was discovered in the Birdless Grove at Goodwood on Monday, the 4th of August.' Who could go on day after day listening to the tale of discarded rubbish? The BBC almost drove us insane during the General Strike with announcements of the hours of departure of railway-trains. But I would rather listen to a BBC announcer reading aloud a Bradshaw of railway-trains than a Bradshaw of rubbish.

Possibly, the scheme might be more effective if, instead of merely giving a description of the rubbish deposited, the name and address of the litter-thrower were made part of the announcement. I should myself feel uneasy if I heard the news being broadcast to the nation that I had been seen throwing the shell of a hard-boiled egg on to the grass of the river-bank near Shillingford Bridge. The BBC would, in such circumstances, have to be exceedingly careful to verify the names of the litter-throwers reported to it. It would never do to announce, without having made the most searching inquiries into the truth of the statement: 'A man was seen furtively throwing a paper-bag into a rhododendron-bush at Abinger Hammer. To the Boy Scout who demanded his name he admitted, under pressure, that he was Mr John Galsworthy.' If this sort of thing were to happen the BBC would soon be spending half its income in defending itself in libel actions. Yet, in order to shame the litter-thrower, we must name the litter-thrower. He has no conscience to which to appeal. If he had, he would not throw litter.

from 'The Militant Rambler' by Robert Lynd

1   Compare the way Robert Lynd has treated his theme with the way that Orwell treated his theme. Discuss how Robert Lynd might have written about litter, if he had used the same style as Orwell used.

2   Writing in the style that Lynd has used is much more difficult than it might appear. It is far easier to parody such a style than it is to write with genuine wit. Bearing this in mind, write an essay poking fun at a feature of our way of life that you regard as ridiculous. When you have finished, read your essays to one another and discuss them critically. Are they genuinely witty or are they merely unsuccessful parodies?

The essay as a personal view

Popular superstitions

Going yesterday to dine with an old acquaintance, I had the misfortune to find his whole family very much dejected. Upon asking him the occasion of it, he told me that his wife had dreamt a strange dream the night before, which they were afraid portended some misfortune to themselves or to their children. At her coming into the room, I observed a settled melancholy in her countenance, which I should have been troubled for, had I not heard from whence it proceeded. We were no sooner sat down, but, after having looked upon me a little while, 'My dear,' says she, turning to her husband, 'you may now see the stranger that was in the candle last night.' Soon after this, as they began to talk of family affairs, a little boy at the lower end of the table told her that he was to go into join-hand on Thursday. 'Thursday!' says she. 'No, child; if it please God, you shall not begin upon Childermas-day; tell your writing master that Friday will be soon enough.' I was reflecting with myself on the oddness of her fancy, and wondering that anybody would establish it as a rule, to lose a day in every week. In the midst of these my musings, she desired me to reach her a little salt upon the point of my knife, which I did in such a trepidation and hurry of obedience, that I let it drop by the way; at which she immediately startled, and said it fell towards her. Upon this I looked very blank; and observing the concern of the whole table, began to consider myself, with some confusion, as a person that had brought a disaster upon the family. The lady, however, recovering herself after a little space, said to her husband with a sigh, 'My dear, misfortunes never come single.' My friend, I found, acted but an under part at his table, and, being a man of more good nature than understanding, thinks himself obliged to fall in with all the passions and humours of his yoke-fellow. 'Do not you remember, child,' says she, 'that the pigeonhouse fell the very afternoon that our careless wench spilt the salt upon the table?' — 'Yes,' says he, 'my dear, and the next post brought us an account of the battle of Almanza.' The reader may guess at the figure I made, after having done all this mischief. I dispatched my dinner as soon as I could, with my usual taciturnity; when to my utter confusion, the lady seeing me quitting my knife and fork, and laying them across one another upon my plate, desired me that I would humour her so far as to take them out of that figure, and place them side by side. What the absurdity was which I had committed I did not know, but I suppose there was some traditionary superstition in it; and therefore, in obedience to the lady of the house, I disposed of my knife and fork in two parallel lines, which is the figure I shall always lay them in for the future, though I do not know any reason for it.

It is not difficult for a man to see that a person has conceived an aversion to him. For my own part, I quickly found, by the lady's looks, that she regarded me as a very odd kind of fellow, with an unfortunate aspect. For which reason I took my leave immediately after dinner, and withdrew to my own lodgings. Upon my return home, I fell into a profound contemplation on the evils that attend these superstitious follies of mankind; how they subject us to imaginary afflictions, and additional sorrows, that do not properly come within our lot. As if the natural calamities of life were not sufficient for it, we turn the most indifferent circumstances into misfortunes, and suffer as much from trifling accidents as from real evils. I have known the shooting of a star spoil a night's rest; and have seen a man in love grow pale, and lose his appetite, upon the plucking of a merry-thought. A screech-owl at midnight has alarmed a family more than a band of robbers; nay, the voice of a cricket hath struck more terror than the roaring of a lion. There is nothing so inconsiderable which may not appear dreadful to an imagination that is filled with omens and prognostics. A rusty nail, or a crooked pin, shoot up into prodigies.

An old maid that is troubled with the vapours produces infinite disturbances of this kind, among her friends and neighbours. I know a maiden aunt of a great family, who is one of these antiquated Sibyls, that forebodes and prophesies from one end of the year to the other. She is always seeing apparitions, and hearing death-watches; and was the other day almost frighted out of her wits by the great house-dog that howled in the stable, at a time when she lay ill of the toothache. Such an extravagant cast of mind engages multitudes of people not only in impertinent terrors, but in supernumerary duties of life; and arises from that fear and ignorance which are natural to the soul of man. The horror with which we entertain the thoughts of death (or indeed of any future evil), and the uncertainty of its approach, fill a melancholy mind with innumerable apprehensions and suspicions, and consequently dispose it to the observation of such groundless prodigies and predictions. For as it is the chief concern of wise men to retrench the evils of life by the reasonings of philosophy; it is the employment of fools to multiply them by the sentiments of superstition.

For my own part, I should be very much troubled were I endowed with this divining quality, though it should inform me truly of everything that can befall me. I would not anticipate the relish of any happiness, nor feel the weight of any misery, before it actually arrives.

I know but one way of fortifying my soul against these gloomy presages and terrors of mind, and that is, by securing to myself the friendship and protection of that Being who disposes of events and governs futurity. He sees, at one view, the whole thread of my existence, not only that part of it which I have already passed through, but that which runs forward into all the depths of eternity. When I lay me down to sleep, I recommend myself to His care; when I awake, I give myself up to His direction. Amidst all the evils that threaten me, I will look up to Him for help, and question not but He will either avert them, or turn them to my advantage. Though I know neither the time nor the manner of the death I am to die, I am not at all solicitous about it; because I am sure that He knows them both, and that He will not fail to comfort and support me under them.

Joseph Addison

1   In the part of Addison's essay dealing with the visit to his friend's house, which details impress us with the feeling that this was a real

situation involving real people? How does he bring alive the atmosphere of the occasion?

2 In his reflections on his experience after returning to his own house, what arguments does he put forward against popular superstitions? How does he retain a sense of personal involvement through the further examples he introduces?

3 Why does he say that he would personally be much troubled were he to be 'endowed with this divining quality'?

4 Look closely at the final paragraph of the essay. In what way does it present a conclusive answer to those of a superstitious nature? How does its change of tone underline the deeply personal quality of Addison's reflections?

5 Structurally, this essay is satisfyingly clear-cut: it consists of a paragraph of lengthy reminiscence incorporating Addison's own amazement at the extent of his friends' superstitions, two paragraphs of further examples and more firmly stated reflections, and finally a summary of his own profound convictions of the matter. Working broadly along the same lines of development write an essay in which you convey your own personal feelings about one of the following topics:

(a) unemployment
(b) old age
(c) wasting time
(d) embarrassment
(e) poverty
(f) food fads
(g) self-indulgence

The essay as tour de force

There is a certain brand of essay which seems intent — before anything else — on impressing us. True, its primary object — like that of some other essays — is to inform the reader, but the method by which its information is communicated is something akin to startling him. Where other essays educate by amusing us or by fixing our attention on the implications of personal experience, this sort works through surprise. The surprise may lie in the subject itself or it may spring from the author's handling of his material. It may derive from the treatment of old ideas in a new way or it may be rooted in novel attitudes on the writer's part.

It is sometimes possible for shaky suppositions or doubtful premises to be made to appear convincing simply by means of the brilliance with which they are presented. Ideas may be bent, if not positively distorted, when treated in this manner. Some readers may feel that such is the case with the essay by Aldous Huxley from which the following extract is taken – but careful study will be necessary before we jump to conclusions:

Comfort

French hotel-keepers call it *Le confort moderne*, and they are right. For comfort is a thing of recent growth, younger than steam, a child when telegraphy was born, only a generation older than radio. The invention of the means of being comfortable and the pursuit of comfort as a desirable end – one of the most desirable that human beings can propose to themselves – are modern phenomena, unparalleled in history since the time of the Romans. Like all phenomena with which we are extremely familiar, we take them for granted, as a fish takes the water in which it lives, not realising the oddity and novelty of them, not bothering to consider their significance. The padded chair, the well-sprung bed, the sofa, central heating, and the regular hot bath – these and a host of other comforts enter into the daily lives of even the most moderately prosperous of the Anglo-Saxon bourgeoisie. Three hundred years ago they were unknown to the greatest kings. This is a curious fact which deserves to be examined and analysed.

The first thing that strikes one about the discomfort in which our ancestors lived is that it was mainly voluntary. Some of the apparatus of modern comfort is of purely modern invention; people could not put rubber tyres on their carriages before the discovery of South America and the rubber plant. But for the most part there is nothing new about the material basis of our comfort. Men could have made sofas and smoking-room chairs, could have installed bathrooms and central heating and sanitary plumbing any time during the last three or four thousand years. And as a matter of fact, at certain periods they did indulge themselves in these comforts. Two thousand years before Christ, the inhabitants of Cnossos were familiar with sanitary plumbing. The Romans had invented an elaborate system of hot-air heating, and the bathing facilities in a smart Roman villa were luxurious and complete beyond the dreams of the modern man. There were sweating-rooms, massage-rooms, cold plunges, tepid drying-rooms with (if we may believe Sidonius Apollinaris) improper frescoes on the walls and comfortable couches where you could lie and talk to your friends. As for the public baths, they were almost inconceivably luxurious. 'To such a height of luxury have we reached,' said Seneca, 'that we are dissatisfied if, in our baths, we do not tread on gems.' The size and completeness of the thermae was proportionable to their splendour. A single room of the baths of Diocletian has been transformed into a large church.

It would be possible to adduce many other examples showing what could be done with the limited means at our ancestors' disposal in the way of making life comfortable. They show sufficiently clearly that if the men of the Middle Ages and early modern epoch lived in filth and discomfort, it was not for any lack or ability to change their mode of life; it was because they chose to live in this way, because filth and discomfort fitted in with their principles and prejudices, political, moral and religious.

What have comfort and cleanliness to do with politics, morals and religion? At a first glance one would say that there was and could be no casual connection between armchairs and democracies, sofas and the relaxation of the family system, hot baths and the decay of Christian orthodoxy. But look more closely and you will discover that there exists the closest connection between the recent growth of comfort and the recent history of ideas. I hope in this essay to make that connection manifest, to show why it was not possible (not materially, but psychologically impossible) for the Italian princes of the quattrocento, for the Elizabethan, even for Louis XIV to live in what the Romans would have called common cleanliness and decency, or enjoy what would be to us indispensable comforts.

Let us begin with the consideration of armchairs. These, I propose to show, only became possible with the breakdown of monarchical and feudal power and the decay of the old family and social hierarchies. Smoking-room chairs and sofas exist to be lolled in. In a well-made modern armchair you cannot do anything but loll. Now, lolling is neither dignified nor respectful. When we wish to appear impressive, when we have to administer a rebuke to an inferior, we do not lie on a deep chair with our feet on the mantelpiece; we sit up and try to look majestical. Similarly, when we wish to be polite to a lady or show respect to the old or eminent, we cease to loll; we stand, or at least we straighten ourselves up. Now, in the past human society was a hierarchy in which every man was always engaged in being impressive towards his inferiors or being respectful to those above him. Lolling in such societies was utterly impossible. It was as much out of the question for Louis XIV to loll in the presence of his courtiers as it was for them to loll in the presence of their king. It was only when he attended a session of the Parlement that the King of France ever lolled in public. On these occasions he reclined in the Bed of Justice, while Princes sat, the great officers of the crown stood, and the smaller fry knelt. Comfort was proclaimed as the appanage of royalty. Only the king might stretch his legs. We may feel sure, however, that he stretched them in a very majestic manner. The lolling was purely ceremonial and accompanied by no loss of dignity. At ordinary times the king was seated, it is true, but seated in a dignified and upright position; the appearance of majesty had to be kept up. (For, after all, majesty is mainly a question of majestical appearance.) The courtiers, meanwhile, kept up the appearances of deference, either standing, or else, if their rank was very high and their blood peculiarly blue, sitting, even in the royal presence, on stools. What was true of the king's court was true of the nobleman's household; and the squire was to his dependents, the merchant was to his apprentices and servants, what the monarch was to his courtiers. In all cases the superior had to express his superiority by being dignified, the inferior his inferiority by being deferential; there could be no lolling. Even in the intimacies of family life it was the same; the parents ruled like popes and princes, by divine right; the children were their subjects. Our fathers took the fifth commandment very seriously – how seriously may be judged from the fact that during the great Calvin's theocratic rule of Geneva a child was publicly decapitated for having ventured to strike its parents. Lolling on the part of children, though not perhaps a capital offence, would have been regarded as an act of the grossest disrespect, punishable by much flagellation, starving and confinement. For a slighter insult – neglect to touch his cap – Vespasiano Gonzaga kicked his only son to death; one shudders to think what he might have been provoked to do if the boy had lolled. If the children might not loll in the presence of their parents, neither might the parents loll in the presence of their children, for fear of demeaning themselves in the eyes of those whose duty it was to honour them. Thus we see that in the European society of two or three hundred years ago it was impossible for any one — from the Holy Roman Emperor and the King of France down to the poorest beggar, from the bearded patriarch to the baby — to loll in the presence of any one else. Old furniture reflects the physical habits of the hierarchical society for which it was made. It was in the power of medieval and renaissance craftsmen to create armchairs and sofas that might have rivalled in comfort those of today. But society being what, in fact, it was, they did nothing of the kind. It was not, indeed, until the sixteenth century that chairs became at all common. Committee-men now loll, Members of Parliament are comfortably seated, but authority still belongs to a Chairman, still issues from a symbolical Chair. In the Middle Ages only the great had chairs. When a great man travelled, he took his chair with him, so that he might never be seen detached from the outward and visible sign of his authority. To this day the Throne no less than the Crown is the symbol of royalty. In medieval times the vulgar sat, whenever it was permissible for them to sit, on benches, stools, and settles. With the rise, during the Renaissance period, of a rich and independent bourgeoisie, chairs began to be more freely used. Those who could afford chairs sat in them, but sat with dignity and discomfort; for the chairs of the sixteenth century were still very throne-like, and imposed upon those who sat in them a painfully majestic attitude. It was only in the eighteenth century, when the old hierarchies were seriously breaking up, that furniture began to be comfortable. And even then there was no real lolling. Armchairs and sofas on which men (and, later, women) might indecorously sprawl, were not made until democracy was firmly established, the middle classes enlarged to gigantic proportions, good manners lost from out of the world, women emancipated, and family restraints dissolved.

from 'Proper Studies' by Aldous Huxley

1   What is the effect of the first two sentences? What do they lead us to expect?

2   What 'curious fact' does Huxley introduce as the central observation of his first paragraph? Is there anything really remarkable about
it?

3   How does he expand on this observation in the second and third
paragraphs? Are the ideas he puts forward here any more extraordinary
than those in the first paragraph? How does he convince us of their
validity? What is the purpose and force of the examples he gives?

4   How does his discussion of armchairs establish and illustrate the
'closest connection' between the recent growth of comfort and the
recent history of ideas? What examples does he give of the rejection of
lolling as a feature of 'the old family and social hierarchies'? Do you feel
any of his examples to be unnecessary or is their cumulative effect
important in the presentation of Huxley's theories?

5   Look at Huxley's outline of the history and importance of the
chair, starting with the words 'it was not, indeed, until the sixteenth
century that chairs became at all common.' Do you think it leads
logically to the assertions he makes in the final sentence of the extract?

6   To what extent do you feel that this essay depends on its author's
wide knowledge and clever manipulation of ideas to make its full effect?
Does it surprise us in the way it presents its central thesis?

7   Write a short assessment of this extract, paying particular attention to the degree of success you feel Huxley achieves in arguing his case.

The study essay

We turn now to consider the business of essay writing as part of the
study of a subject. If you are studying 'arts' subjects, you will be
particularly familiar with this often very demanding exercise but it is
likely that an occasional essay is regarded as an essential part of the study
of whatever subject you are taking. It is a vital tool in furthering your
mastery of the discipline of thought appropriate to your subject. What
do we mean by 'a discipline of thought' and what are the mental
processes involved in writing a study essay?

Analysis and Synthesis

The study of a subject means confronting a mass of details, facts, or ideas
and, with the aid of books and teachers, working towards perceiving an
order in them. There are two fundamental thought processes involved
in discovering this order: we *analyse* the mass of material by breaking it
down into smaller details relevant to the specified topic and we *synthesise*
or make general statements about these details. The general statements

bring out what the details have in common and enable us to see them in a more coherent pattern. Our analysis may involve sorting the details, facts or ideas into categories and also perceiving cause and effect among them.

What may go wrong in writing a study essay?

Whatever your subject, the main problems in writing an adequate essay are likely to fall within one or more of these three categories:—

1   Inadequate treatment of details or inclusion of irrelevant details — the essay may be little more than a sequence of unsupported generalisations.

2   Inadequate development of generalisations; that is to say, failure to synthesise and relate the material to the topic or question on which you are writing.

3   Failure to achieve a good balance between the details or examples in the essay and the generalised thinking that organises the material, in other words, a failure to structure the essay.

These difficulties are examined further in the following three sections, each of which contains an essay written by a student studying an Advanced Level subject.

Including sufficient analysis of detail

'Critically evaluate the use of the questionnaire and different interview techniques in social surveys.'

When a sociologist wishes to obtain information from a group of people or a community, then the most common method of obtaining this information is with the use of a questionnaire. The simplest one to use is the mail questionnaire which is posted to the group of people who are to be questioned and it then can be easily returned to the base where the study is taking place. There are a number of different forms in which these questionnaires can come and each has its different problems and uses.

Other forms of survey are interviews where the interviewer actually talks face-to-face with the person being interviewed. The problem with this method is the time taken and also the greater expense involved but the advantages are that greater detail can be extracted and certain points can be elaborated.*

Another form of social survey is participant observation. This form of survey involves a person working or living with a group of people so as to obtain information. The advantage of this method is that he can become friendly with the people he is mixing with and therefore obtain much more information. The problem again with this sort of survey is the time it takes and the expense. Also, in this type of survey, the outsider must not become too involved with any one group so as to take sides, as it would not then be an objective survey.

Often, before a major survey is started, a pilot survey takes place before it. This involves about 10 per cent. of the whole group to be surveyed and it can give the sociologist a rough idea of the results of the whole group to be questioned.

One of the most well-known questionnaires is the census which takes place every ten years. The information is analysed and used by the Registrar General and almost the exact population of the country can be worked out. There is often controversy over the census because the questions are thought to be too personal.

On the whole it seems that no one form of social survey can be said to be better than another, as a questionnaire may be suitable in one case and yet an interview may be necessary in another.

This simple essay was written in the first few weeks of a student's Advanced Level Sociology course. The teacher marking it pointed out a number of places in the essay where insufficient detail had been included. It was not possible for the student to make any very telling criticisms of surveying techniques because he had not analysed those techniques adequately. For example, at *, the teacher wrote, 'You need to examine different interview techniques – formal/informal etc.' Where else in this essay do you think the student should have provided more detail in explanation of his generalisations?

Developing generalisations
'Compare the importance of minerals in the economics of Ghana and Liberia.'

Ghana is a relatively prosperous country and is certainly one of the most developed economically in the whole of West Africa. Mining in Ghana is mainly carried out by large foreign companies. This is because the Africans were originally unable to provide the huge amounts of capital and techniques required for modern deep mining.

In Ghana there are four main minerals: gold, manganese, bauxite and diamonds. Gold gave the country its former name and was originally of high importance. The main area is in the south-west. Deep mining operations centre about the towns of Tarkwa, Prestea, Kononge and, most importantly, Obuasi. Gold today accounts for one tenth of the country's total exports. Deep mining accounts for 90 per cent of all gold mining in Ghana. Exports of gold have increased: the annual export was 300 000 fine ounces at the beginning of the century but today it is 800 000 fine ounces.

Manganese, unlike gold, is mined open-cast at Nsuta, forty miles north of Takoradi. Ghana used to be far more important as a manganese producer but now it is only a moderate producer. It is far less important to Ghana than gold is.

Diamonds are worked near Kade in the Birim valley by European companies. However, Africans work deposits in the Bonsa valley. By weight alone, Ghana is the leading producer of diamonds but not by value since its diamonds are mostly small and discoloured.

The fourth major mineral is bauxite, the ore of aluminium. This is quarried at Awaso. The Volta Dam and power station were completed in 1965 and most of the power produced is used by an aluminium smelter at Tema, initially using imported alumina. Ghana should become a major producer of aluminium, most of which is exported.

As can be seen, minerals are quite important to Ghana and account for quite a high percentage of its total exports.

Liberia depends even more heavily on its mineral wealth than does Ghana. Its only important mineral is iron, which is of high quality. This was first mined in the Bomi Hills, forty-five miles north-west of Monrovia, and on the Mano river. A mineral railway brings the ore to Monrovia. Other large deposits have been developed on Mount Nimba, from where a 170-mile railway takes the ore to the specially constructed deep-water port of Buchanan. A fourth deposit is quarried in the Bong Hills.

Iron ore accounts for as much as 75 per cent of Liberian exports. Over 25 million tons are exported in a year and there are substantial reserves outside the four mining areas, so the long-term prospects are good. Rubber used to be Liberia's most important export, accounting for 97 per cent of its exports, but that figure has now been reduced to 20 per cent, entirely because of iron.

There is clearly no absence of detailed knowledge in this essay. The student has produced his material in a clear and orderly manner. What he has failed to do is to rise to an effective synthesis of the material; he has not produced generalisations comparing and contrasting the importance of minerals in the economies of these two countries. Discuss the following questions:

(a) The teacher marking this essay wrote at the end of it, 'I have underlined the only *comparative* statement you have made in the whole essay.' Identify this comparative statement.

(b) He further wrote, 'Do not leave the reader to do all the answering of the question by inference/deduction from your factual content.' Where in the course of this essay do you consider that general comparative statements should have been made?

(c) Review the content of this essay. Working from the material the student has included, make some generalisations about the relative importance of minerals in the economies of Ghana and Liberia.

Structuring your essay

In preparing to write an essay, it is unlikely that you would be pursuing the two thought processes of *analysis* and *synthesis* entirely independently: you would more often be working away at analysing the main elements in the subject and synthesising them into generalisations at the same time. However, by the time you come to write, you should have a rough idea of the sort of synthesis which will enable you to put the facts into perspective and create an orderly interpretation. You might well begin your essay by stating this tentative synthesis and then proceed to analyse the facts, examining each aspect of the subject in turn whilst keeping the tentative synthesis in mind. If everything falls neatly into place within the overall interpretation, then you would naturally conclude by restating the generalisation more firmly. If, however, you are thinking freshly and in an exploratory way about your subject, then it is likely that certain aspects of the subject will assume a greater importance than you had expected and that, as you analyse the material in the course of writing your essay, you will gradually modify your original idea. The concluding generalisation or synthesis may therefore be different from the tentative generalisation from which your essay departed.

We have described a simple essay structure which might be represented by the following diagram:

tentative synthesis
↓
analysis of the facts or substance of the essay
↓
firmer or modified synthesis

If the essay topic is presented in the form of a question to which there may be alternative answers, for example, *Is Othello Noble?*, a slightly different structure will be necessary. In this example, the answer may be summarised as, 'Yes but . . . . 'or 'No but . . . . ' and you will certainly be asking what the word 'noble' may imply. The essay might, therefore, begin with an examination and definition of the question in terms with which you can deal. It might proceed by offering alternative interpretations based on close examination of the evidence and it would then conclude by weighing up the different possibilities and relating them back to the question. Such an essay structure may be represented by this diagram:

examination and redefinition of the question
↓
provision of evidence for one possible synthesis
↓
provision of evidence for alternative synthesis
↓
weighing up of evidence in the light of the question

A third type of structure will be appropriate for the topic which requires you to compare and contrast two aspects of a subject. The essay on minerals in Africa in the previous section is a good example. Here the preparatory work is particularly important for you will need to classify the material under appropriate headings which refer to both sides of the question. In the case of minerals in Ghana and Liberia, the headings might include: main minerals in both countries; location and transport arrangements in both countries; history of attendant industrial development in both countries. Having thus classified your material, you are in a position to start the essay by presenting a survey of the aspects of the topic that you intend to cover, i.e. a statement of your classified headings. You would then deal with each aspect in turn and conclude with an overall synthesis which directly answers the question. The scheme might, therefore, be:

statement of aspects of topic to be analysed
↓
analysis of one aspect + comparative generalisation
↓
analysis of second aspect + comparative generalisation
(and of further aspects until the topic is covered)
↓
overall comparison or synthesis

In the light of these three possible structures for essays, and bearing in mind that many modifications of these structures may be appropriate, discuss the following essay. Where has the writer made generalisations? Where has he analysed his material? Do you think he has structured his essay appropriately? Which of the above schemes does it most closely correspond to? Can you suggest any ways in which the structure might be improved? Take some of your own essays and analyse them together in a similar way.

Is man a pest?

A dictionary definition of a pest would be — a troublesome or destructive person, animal or thing. Man can therefore be a pest in that he is an animal, but is he troublesome or destructive? This question must be answered in order to determine whether man is a pest.

In certain cases man is not a pest. Man has built around him his own habitat. By doing so he allowed 'opportunists' to enter his environment and if it suited them then they would stay. Man maintained the constant environment for them. He cleared vast areas of forest forming an 'open habitat'. In these regions the weeds that we know today began to spring up. In forests they could not grow because the trees shaded them from the sunlight. Weeds are 'opportunists'. Man built houses and towns. Into these environments moved animals such as mice, rats, spiders, cock-roaches, because here they could collect food remnants left by man. Often, however, these 'opportunists' cause man hardship, by bringing disease. Even so all these organisms, animal and plant, could not survive as well as they do if man was not around.

Man has also domesticated certain animals and cultivated certain plants. These organisms are described as cultigens.

Without man corn as it now exists in its cultivated form could not survive. Man must husk the ears and plant the kernels. Other plants have also been cultivated but man is not a herbivore. He has always had a taste for meat. So he domesticated pigs, sheep, cows. These he feeds on grain or grass which he himself has grown. Agreed, he kills these cultigens for food for himself, but while they are alive they live a very easy life being in no competition for food. Man has created this system so that he is no longer involved in competition for food himself. He has become a first or second order consumer. He has erected fences to keep out the wolves, invented insecticides to remove insects. These animals would if allowed join a competition they create, for the food that man had provided. However, insecticides such as DDT can lead to serious consequences for man and similar organisms towards the top of food chains. The insecticides become more and more concentrated as we go up a food chain such as that of insects – songbirds – sparrowhawk. In Britain, this particular case became so bad that the sparrowhawk population became almost zero.

Man, or his children especially, have the idea of keeping 'pets'. They are kept mainly for amusement or affection and include such animals as budgerigars, cats, hamsters, parrots or such plants as cacti. These organisms are maintained, given free life, with no competition. They are not killed for our own needs generally, and without man they would have a job to survive.

Throughout human history man has collected things. These include such articles as poisons, paints or wool (for clothes). In some cases man has had to kill the organism to get what he wants, as in the example of the fisher in North America. However, his collection in this instance resulted in very adverse affects to man himself. The fisher is a weasel-like animal which had a very valuable fur. Man trapped it for its fur and practically wiped it out. But the fisher was a predator on porcupines, its weasel-like body enabling it to swim under the quills and attack the porcupine from beneath. Once it was wiped out, there was no natural enemy to keep the porcupine population in check. The vast numbers of porcupine now chew their way through valuable forest lands. Man's misadventure was disastrous for the fisher, but very advantageous for the porcupine.

Man has many 'parasites'. These include such things as the virus which causes the common cold, endo parasites of the gut, for example some bacteria, taenia, bacteria which cause cholera, tuberculosis, the fungus which causes athletes foot, the flukes of the Trematoda (Platyhelminthes) and insects, for example body lice. Without man they would not exist today.

Man, once he got a strong foot-hold on this planet, grew quickly in numbers. In recent years this has been termed the 'population explosion'. By doing so, he has had to create more of his environment from the environment that originally existed. This means that those not dependent on man are suffering. An example of this is the orang-utan of the forests of Borneo. Of course, as man increases in numbers so food becomes shorter and shorter mainly for man but for other animals as well.

Pollution is another problem upon life caused by man. All organisms produce waste, but that from those other than man forms the food of another. Man, present in such large numbers and concentrated in cities, produces too much sewage for ordinary biological methods of removal. It is dumped into rivers, lakes, harbours or the sea, and can destroy the cleansing abilities of the water and kill the native organisms. Industrial pollution is probably worse still. Chemical by-products are pumped into the air, forming smog which is a serious health risk, or into streams destroying waterfowl, fish and vegetation. Dumps have been formed of all kinds of waste, from plastic cups to drums of chemical waste, which not only look unpleasant but can be and often are highly dangerous. These pollution problems are minimal when compared to those caused by nuclear power. Atomic explosions spew out radiation over vast areas and peaceful uses in the production of atomic energy, result in the production of radioactive waste as well.

From this essay it appears that man is a pest to some organisms but not to others. But I think that man the agriculturist was not a pest to living organisms as a whole, whereas man the industrialist is. I hope that man the ecologist will come next with his wisdom and sort out this mess of a planet that man has created for himself.

5 Journalism

Reports

Reports and articles in the press — regardless of their subject matter — frequently bear the stylistic stamp or hallmark of the journal in which they appear. Where the more staid, established papers will usually endeavour to present their news in as restrained and objective a manner as possible, their popular, tabloid counterparts may well treat identical material more freely, employing the kind of tone and adding the sort of comment which their readership has come to expect of them. Here, for example, is the way in which two London newspapers — *The Times* and *The Daily Mirror* — reported on a speech made in Chicago about the trends in British and American English by the chief editor of the Oxford English Dictionaries.

Britons and Americans are growing words apart

Chicago, June 27
English-speaking Americans and English-speaking Britons will not be able to understand each other in another 200 years, according to the world's acknowledged authority on English English.

Language differences between the two countries have been growing steadily since the American colonists got rid of the British in 1776, Mr Robert Burchfield, chief editor of the Oxford English Dictionaries, said at a press conference here, and things will get a lot worse.

The term 'English speaking peoples' would become obsolete; schools would have to decide whether to teach 'British English' or 'American English'; and vocabulary, not accent, would be the main stumbling block to communication across the Atlantic.

'The two forms of English are in a state of dissimilarity now which should, on my forecast, lead to a condition of unintelligibility given another 200 years', Mr Burchfield said.

Part of the blame for the language drift lay with British academics who refused to have any dealings with American English, he said.

Mr Burchfield said the language split began in the late eighteenth century. 'We are at the halfway point, with dissimilarity which is noticeable to any man, woman or child,' he added.

The differences were not much more than jokes at the moment: the British lift versus the American elevator and the expression to 'knock someone up', which in the United States meant to make a woman pregnant.

He estimated that 47 million of the 50 million Britons had never visited the United States and that 200 million of the 220 million Americans had never visited Britain. 'The language is governed by those 200 million and those 47 million,' he said.

'Broadly speaking, British English is retaining its more ancient character and American English is changing.'

British English of the future would be easier to learn because it would be less diverse. Differences between the two Englishes would intensify as time went on. Mr Burchfield said, however, that he rejected the 'ancient belief' that there was or should be only one form of English.

from 'The Times' 28 June 1978

It'll all be US to us

Americans and Britons will not be able to understand one another's languages by the end of the next 200 years, an expert on the English language claimed yesterday.

By that time American English will have become so different from British English that the two nations will no longer share a common language.

The prediction was made by Robert Burchfield, chief editor of the Oxford English Dictionaries.

Burchfield, who was speaking in Chicago, picked out a couple of the more familiar examples of transatlantic differences in definitions.

A British lift is an American elevator. If you 'knock someone up' in Britain you wake him to go to work; if you do it in America you make a girl pregnant.

But there are more serious examples.

An Englishman who asks the friendly stranger in a New York bar whether he's got a fag is more likely to get a black eye than a cigarette. In American English a fag is a homosexual.

Burchfield blames the split between the two languages on British academics who refuse to have any dealings with American English.

But he didn't mention the fact that the rest of us don't live in ivory towers. So we absorb the current language of Manhattan and Los Angeles through a steady series of lessons on television.

It didn't take long for us to learn to say 'No way' instead of 'Not likely'.

One threat to both varieties of English is gobbledygook.

Burchfield himself managed to use that when he said: 'The two forms of English are in a *state of dissimilarity* now which should lead, on my forecast, to a *condition of unintelligibility* given another 200 years.'

David Bradbury from 'The Daily Mirror' 28 June 1978

1   How much comment, as opposed to purely objective reporting, does each of these articles contain? What is the nature and purpose of such comment? What does it reflect of the writer's attitude to Robert Burchfield's speech? Is it possible to draw any conclusions about the sort of journalism practised in *The Times* and *The Daily Mirror* from this sort of comparison of the two articles?

2   To what extent do the vocabulary and illustrations employed in the two pieces serve to reinforce the distinction between them?

3   Does either article appear to you to be more obviously informative than its counterpart? Does either seem more entertaining? What conclusions can you draw from your observations?

4   In both reports, the heading takes the form of a pun. Can you analyse and explain the pun in each case? To what extent is each heading appropriate to the general tone of the article above which it appears?

5   Using *The Times* and *Daily Mirror* reports as your models, prepare and write parallel articles on either (a) a recent local news item which has caught your imagination; or (b) an imaginary happening suggested by one of the following headlines:
(i)**Back to Subnormal** (ii)**Don't Look Now!** (iii)**The Best of Enemies**

Reports and editorials

In a news report the aim of the writer is to give information to the reader. His purpose should be to present the facts clearly and concisely without commenting on them. A typical newspaper report follows a set pattern. It begins with one or two sentences, which summarise and themselves contain all the most important facts. These are then developed and more fully explained in the paragraphs that follow and further less important facts are added. This structure is used, since a newspaper report often has to be shortened, if the space available for it is suddenly reduced at the last moment, because another more important news story comes in. If news reports are written in this way, then a sub-editor can shorten them very quickly, by cutting out the final paragraphs, since he knows that these are the least important ones. A good news report should be objective and unbiased, yet, as we have already seen in the previous section, the way a reporter arranges and presents his information means that the same event can be reported in a number of very different styles and from a wide variety of angles.

Editorials are written in a very subjective style. The purpose of the editorial writer is to comment upon a particular issue raised by one of the news reports. He is concerned to express a point of view and to develop an argument, rather than to convey information. The nature of the editorials in a particular paper varies according to the paper's general policy and the readership to which it is designed to appeal.

Tobacco firms and smokers face new curbs

A major new offensive against smoking – described by Mr Ennals, Social Services Secretary, as 'the major cause of premature death in Britain' – was launched by the Government yesterday.

Cigarette packets will carry a tougher health warning, advertising of 'high tar' brands will be stopped, and there will be a new crackdown on smoking in public places.

The warning on packets will now read 'Smoking can *seriously* damage your health' – adding the word seriously – and it will be called a Government Health Department's warning.

Mr Ennals also foreshadowed a new tax on cigarettes scientifically assessed as the most harmful.

In a speech on preventive medicine in London, he appealed to

Britain's 19 million cigarette smokers: 'Stop the habit.' He added: 'You feel better. You smell better. You taste better. And you have cash for other things.'

Mr Ennals announced that:

Cigarette packets will carry a stronger health warning that Smoking can 'seriously' damage health.

Advertising of cigarettes in the 'high tar' group will be stopped immediately and of the 'middle to high tar' group by the end of next year. Adverts will concentrate on the two lowest tar groups. Manufacturers have agreed to try to eliminate all 'high' brands after two years and to introduce no new 'high' or 'middle to high' in the meantime.

Britain has proposed to the Common Market that cigarettes should be taxed according to their health danger.

There will be a new crackdown on smoking in public places, and the Health Education Council is to get an extra £1 million to put over the anti-smoking message, especially to the young.

The Government's aim was to discourage non-smokers from getting into the habit, persuade smokers to stop or switch to less damaging brands, and to create 'a non-smoking environment' with facilities for those who wished to smoke, rather than vice versa, said Mr Ennals.

He and Mr Roland Moyle, Minister of State, had sought the co-operation of the tobacco industry and the progress made was 'significant'.

According to the Tobacco Research Council, the average tar yield of cigarettes sold in Britain had been almost halved in the past two years, said Mr Ennals.

Mr Ennals said he wanted to regulate the sponsorship of sporting events by tobacco companies, which he considered both 'grotesque' and an evasion of the spirit of the ban on television advertising. This was still being considered.

He would also be approaching organisations with requests for them to restrict or ban smoking in the public areas they manage. These will include railways and tube trains, buses, airports, cinemas, theatres, concert halls, public buildings, waiting rooms and shops.

In hospitals, smoking should normally be forbidden except in special places, and new guidance issued by his Department pointed out it was essential that patients did not see health professionals smoking.

Mr Ennals rebuffed the argument that if people wanted to take the risks involved in smoking, it was their private concern, and nothing to do with the Government.

Cigarette smoking was now the major cause of premature deaths each year. 'Lung cancer kills 36,000 of them – that's one every fifteen minutes,' he said.

The new campaign was condemned by Action on Smoking and Health (ASH) as a 'weak package which makes almost every conceivable concession to the tobacco industry.'

David Loshak from 'The Daily Telegraph' 9 March 1977

1   List what you consider to be the six most important pieces of information conveyed in this report. Compare your lists and discuss any differences between them.

2   The *Daily Telegraph* chose to report Mr Ennals's speech in detail. Another newspaper might have chosen to report it in much less detail. Using your lists as a basis, produce a news report of Mr Ennals's speech, which is no more than 150 words long.

3   You are the producer of a TV news programme. How would you present a report on the speech in your programme? What visuals would you include to accompany the spoken report? Produce a script giving details of the pictures you would transmit, as well as the text of the report that the newsreader would present.

4   If you were a journalist interviewing Mr Ennals either on TV or for a newspaper, following his speech, what questions would you ask him? In pairs, make a list of your questions and then improvise the interview. Finally, choose one person to take the part of Mr Ennals and act out a press conference at which he answers questions from a number of reporters. Using what is said at the press conference, produce your own newspaper reports and compare them.

5   How sensational is the *Daily Telegraph*'s report of Mr Ennals's speech? How could it have been made more sensational? Think of a sensational headline and draft a more sensational report of the speech.

6   Study the structure of the report. Notice how the main points are encapsulated in the first three paragraphs. What further details that amplify each of these points are added later in the report?

7   Look at the final paragraph. Consider how another reporter might have taken this as his main point and written a report on the

speech from a quite different angle. Write a report on the speech using a headline such as 'Anti-Smoking Organisation Condemns Weak Package'.

The following editorial appeared in the same edition of the *Daily Telegraph*.

The Great Smoking War

Mr Ennals is intensifying the anti-smoking terror campaign. Cigarette packets already proclaim that 'smoking can damage your health'. The word 'seriously' will soon be inserted before 'damage' — 'a significant step forward,' in Mr Ennals's view. Other significant steps forward are planned to eradicate smoking from railways, tube trains, buses, airports, cinemas, theatres, concert halls, public buildings, waiting rooms, hospitals and shops: 'our long term aim must be its eventual disappearance.' As a result, we shall all '*feel* better . . . *smell* better . . . *taste* better' (Mr Ennals's italics) and 'have cash for other things'. What Mr Ennals would do for cash if we all suddenly gave up smoking is obscure. At present smokers pay for about one-third of the Health Service. Presumably he would have to tax 'other things'.

We may assume that Mr Ennals is himself a non-smoker rather than a humbug. He may smell better as a result, but does he think better? His unbalanced and illiberal tirade hardly suggests so. What is 'grotesque', except to him, about tobacco companies sponsoring harmless sports? Should he not rejoice at this tribute paid by vice to virtue? And where, except in his own mind, is the logical connection between the freedom to smoke and the freedom to 'get run over'? We choose to smoke or not, without obviously endangering the lives of others by our choice; few of us choose to get run over, or even claim the right to run over others. Agreed: smoking can damage your health. So can anxiety, which smoking is said to alleviate and Mr Ennals certainly exacerbates. Many, especially creative people, find it difficult or impossible to work without smoking. Giving it up might mean for them less cash for other things, not more. 'By heating vices to much,' wrote Burke, 'they come to love men too little'. The whole anti-smoking campaign runs this risk.

from 'The Daily Telegraph'

1   What is the effect of the headline? Why is the word 'war' used? Suggest alternative headlines that have the same effect.

2   Discuss how the writer mounts an attack on Mr Ennals and his proposals in the first paragraph.

3   What arguments does he put forward in the second paragraph to support his view that Mr Ennals's speech was an 'unbalanced and illiberal tirade'?

4   On what grounds does the writer criticise the whole anti-smoking campaign?

5   How effective is this editorial in conveying the writer's point of view? Compare its structure with that of the report, and discuss the effectiveness of particular words and phrases that the writer uses in order to pour scorn on Mr Ennals and his suggestions.

Reporting and commenting

Many newspaper reports go beyond simple relaying of factual matter concerning a news item. They may include additional background material and even some evaluation of the item of news. The reporter's own reaction may also be implied in the tone he uses to report events. Consider the following report of a debate in the House of Commons.

Ever onward! Rhubarbing on T.V. next?

Not content with parliament being broadcast on the radio, various MPs yesterday urged that there should be no further delay in proceedings being televised.

There were also suggestions that the radio extracts be made longer.

Many MPs clearly believed, then, that there were all sorts of untapped markets for their deliberations.

Where will this lead us? Will proceedings occasionally be adapted for ballet: or come to resemble one of those long-running theatrical entertainments largely designed for Japanese business-men. ('No Sense, Please. We're Backbenchers')

'We must go forward,' Mr Kenneth Lewis (C., Rutland) told the House, 'so the public can see what they hear.'

What joys await the public! Instead of merely hearing them rhubarbing, you will be able to see them doing it. Many members would not rest until this new blow has been struck for democracy.

Some, however, held aloof from the tide of progress.

They included the magnificently-crusty Mr John Stokes (C., Halesowen). If people were guns, Mr Stokes would be a blunderbuss. He may lack the absolute accuracy of these newfangled Gatling guns, but his fire gets home to his own satisfaction.

Mr Stokes is sceptical about all the latest inventions. He is said to entertain the gravest doubts about the effect, on character-building, of the wheel.

Among the furtive, computer-built politicians who litter the Tory benches nowadays, Mr Stokes is a superbly confident and wholesome figure.

He has no intention of tampering with his principles to make them acceptable to the fatuous young-marrieds on suburban housing estates who are supposed to hold the key to elections.

Broadcasting of the House had been a disaster, Mr Stokes believed. 'Prime Minister's Question Time is rapidly degenerating into a farce . . . there is a total lack of dignity now. We do not set a good example of behaviour.'

Many Labour members were only MPs because it kept them off street corners, he admirably observed.

Mr Rooker (Lab., Perry Bar) — who would be at home both as a Labour MP and on a street corner — called out: 'He's out to get on the radio in the morning. That's why he's doing this.'

Mr Stokes ignored him and proceeded on his stately way. The House should have the opportunity of another vote on broadcasting, he said. 'Otherwise we shall sink deeper and deeper into the mire, and the public will despise us.'

Mr Philip Whitehead (Lab., Derby N.), a former television producer, disagreed with Mr Stokes. Mr Whitehead is an intellectual. This means, in practice, that he has a beard and that he refers, as he did yesterday, to 'the electronic media' when he means radio and telly.

Therefore, there seems no point in being an intellectual. His speeches usually just consist of the familiar routine about our living in a diminishing, ever-changing technological world. Anyone could deliver them.

From his remarks yesterday, we gathered that there should be less emphasis in the broadcasts on the exciting bits of the day's business such as Prime Minister's Questions. He thus appeared to be arguing that the public should be hearing more of the boring bits. This was not very persuasive.

Frank Johnson from 'The Daily Telegraph'

1   What is the issue being reported in this article? What arguments are given for and against the proposal? To what extent is this report a straight-forward, orderly presentation of the issue?

2   What is the function of the first three paragraphs? How do they differ from the rest of the article?

3   How would you describe the effect of the fourth paragraph? In what way does it establish the tone for the rest of the report?

4   What is the effect of Frank Johnson's use of such phrases as 'untapped markets', 'this new blow struck for democracy' or 'held aloof from the tide of progress'? Why does the use of these phrases appear humorous in their specific contexts? Can you find other examples of similarly humorous usage of well-known phrases in the report?

5   The reporter offers us some impressions of the MPs who spoke on this issue. Consider his comments on them and notice how much of the report they occupy. For what purpose are they included in the article?

6   To what extent is this a serious piece of reporting? Frank Johnson does not openly express a view on the issue but does he imply an attitude towards it?

Features

A feature article is one that focuses upon a particular topic, person, place or event. Whereas a news reporter writes about an event that has just occurred, a feature writer selects a subject that is considered to be of general interest to the readership of the magazine or newspaper, and writes about it in the way that he thinks will most interest his readers. The type of features that a newspaper or magazine carries will vary according to the nature of the publication and the readership for which it is intended. Similarly, the way a subject is presented will differ according to the newspaper's or magazine's editorial policy. The writer of a features article may be writing to inform his readership, to entertain them, to try to influence them by presenting a convincing argument or by slanting his article in a particular direction, or to stimulate further thought by presenting material that will shock or provoke. The style that the feature writer adopts will depend upon his subject, upon the publication in which his article is to appear and upon what his intention is.

A man's place is in the home

By all the usual standards by which we have come to gauge liberal meetings, this was a relatively mouse-like affair. There were about thirty people there, aged between twenty-five and thirty-five. Some had babies and young children in tow. The small hotel they had taken over for their two-and-a-half day conference rang to demands for a better deal in crossing the sexual barriers. They wanted less discrimination at work, the resolving of sexual roles in the home and even some sort of demarcation in the marriage bed.

What lifted this liberation meeting out of the ordinary and into the extraordinary was that all the people there were men. The entire weekend, down to the last nappy-changing participant, was an all-male affair. The meeting was held recently by the newly-formed Swedish Male Liberation Movement.

It is a rapidly growing organisation of ten to fifteen loose-knit groups, consisting at present of mainly professional and other middle-class males. The groups have sprung up in various parts of Sweden. They are now closing ranks to save the male psyche from what they see as usurping forces, and they are gathering supporters for an offensive which will give a new twist to the battle of the sexes. The groups are also campaigning to free fellow males from the conventional yoke as the family breadwinner, tied to long hours by the career ladder or the contingencies of the job, at the expense of their families.

If the very thought of a male liberation movement strikes any fully paid-up chauvinistic pigs in Britain as amusing or slightly effete, at least the movement is being taken seriously by Swedish doctors and social workers. Among them is Mr Carl Boethius, chairman of Riksforbundet for Sexuell Upplysning, roughly equivalent to our Family Planning Association.

Mr Boethius, was one of the leading speakers at the conference. 'There has been a big change in the Swedish woman's identity, her sexual role, and her personality in recent years. She is feeling strong, confident and a big success in her job. But there is another side, too.

'Swedish husbands are not as dominant as they were fifteen years ago as a result. Buying a new car and house, or just planning a weekend – it was once the husband who decided. Now it is the wife. Yet for the man there has not been much difference, except for that. His role has not changed to the same extent. But if he doesn't change now, his whole life will be one of suffering.'

By all accounts, there is undoubtedly suffering already on a wide scale. The working wife's financial independence means that leaving her partner (many do not formally marry) is often more a question of the problems of flat-hunting than anything else. She often earns more than her husband, for a start.

But even more complex are the changing sexual mores. 'Some of the men who came to the meeting confirm that women are now taking the initiative in sex as well as in everything else in life,' said Mr Boethius. 'This can cause impotence at times in males. There are some complaints to doctors by men who are losing their self-image, their gender identity, because of female liberation.'

Even at work a man cannot escape the feminine revolution. Seven out of ten wives have their own jobs, and there are only 700 000 fewer women than men in the country's workforce of four million. Soon women will be level pegging, it is forecast. Shift work and 'flexi-hours' are widespread so a Swedish father frequently switches to the female role at home to dress, feed and bath the children.

The mixed-up dad situation that sometimes results is illustrated by researchers who recently prepared a major report for the Prime Minister on changing sex roles. The study reveals that the role of man is undergoing a process of transformation – some might say reversal in Sweden. 'Shift workers, those on sick leave, the unemployed and even divorced men exhibit a pent-up capacity for intimacy with the children and for housework,' the report proclaims. Yet there were also a number of cases of males who felt they were losing their manhood; they did not feel 'the man of the house' any more. 'I'm not allowed to say what I think,' confessed one. Another, whose wife wanted another baby, complained: 'I couldn't go through it all again.'

There is still confusion among the 'liberating' males themselves as to what they are really fighting for. The movement seems to attract two sorts. There are those who feel that women have penetrated their world quite far enough and want to call a halt. But there are others, possibly the majority, who wish to emulate the emancipation and improved lifestyle of women, particularly in regard to work.

For some of these male libbers, a husband and father's place is in the home, just as much as it is for their wives. Erik Sidenbladh, a thirty-year-old journalist on Sweden's daily paper *Svenska Dagbladet*, is one of the leaders of a Stockholm group of male liberationists.

'We are fighting the system in which employers push men into a male role of working long hours at the expense of their families, while accepting that a woman can choose not to.'

Erik, whose wife Eva, thirty-one, also works, takes turn with her in looking after their son of seven and daughter aged four, and in shopping and cooking the family meals. 'This is a man's right,' he declares. Not surprisingly, Eva agrees.

Since Mr Boethius feels the movement is likely to spread in Western countries, particularly to Britain, I asked if he had any advice that male liberationists could pass on. 'Man has to learn to adapt to his new role – it can strengthen his marriage rather than destroy it,' he replied. Males must also learn to express their emotions more, and particularly to change the tradition of Nordic 'silent suffering' (or British 'stiff upper lip'), possibly even shedding tears in adversity. 'It is not weak for men to cry,' he added.

In other words, since they cannot obviously beat women, males will *have* to join them. One boy, on learning his father was campaigning for male liberation, asked: 'Are you going to burn your underpants?'

Michael Jeffries from 'The Sunday Times' 29 March 1977

For discussion

1 What do you learn from this article about the Swedish Male Liberation Movement? What is the writer's attitude towards the Movement? Quote from the article to support your answer.

2 What do you think the writer's purpose is? to inform? to entertain? to influence? to provoke further thought?

3 Make a flow-chart to show the order in which the information and views in the article are presented. Discuss how the order could be changed and how the article could be structured differently. What would be the effect of presenting the material in a different order?

4 Is any of the material in the article redundant? Would it lose any of

its impact if it were reduced in length? Discuss which parts you would omit, if you had to shorten it to a third of its length, then rewrite it reducing it to this length. Compare your versions. Who do you think has produced the most effective shortened version? Why do you consider it to be better than the others?

5   Discuss the title of the article. What difference would it make if the title of the article was 'Are you going to burn your underpants?' What other titles can you suggest? Discuss the effect that each one has.

For study and research

Look at a number of different newspapers. Compare their features pages. What differences do you notice? How do you explain these differences? Study the articles in a selection of (a) women's magazines (b) teenage magazines (c) Sunday colour supplements. What differences in content, style and presentation are there? Which articles are the most informative? the most entertaining? the most sensational? Which of the articles that you read did you think was the best written article? Explain why.

For writing

1   You work for a 'popular' newspaper. Using the factual information in the article, *A man's place is in the home*, write a sensational article on this subject. Your chief aim is to capture and hold your reader's attention, rather than to inform or influence him.

2   Write an editorial either supporting the people who have launched the Swedish Male Liberation Movement and suggesting that they must be taken seriously, or pouring scorn on them and ridiculing their views.

3   Write a feature about either your school or your neighbourhood for your local newspaper.

4   Write an article for a magazine about a sport, hobby or activity that interests you.

5   Choose a person, a place or an event that interests you and write a feature article designed to inform your readers about the person, the place or the event.

6   Choose one of the following topics and write a feature article on it: Examinations, The latest fashions, Hitch-hiking, Part-time jobs, Gambling, Collecting things, Conservation, Television, Advertising, Pollution. Research the topic in the way that a feature writer would, before you write your article.

The named column

Most newspapers run a regular column in which the same contributor comments on the ways of the world. In such articles, the writer has a certain licence to 'sound off', to express and develop his personal opinions in a forceful way. He does not necessarily express the official position of the newspaper on any particular issue. Rather he tends to attempt to stir up controversy and to present an original, personal slant on a much-debated topic. He is also likely to present a sociological comment on the state of things generally rather than a critique of a specific newsworthy occurence. There is an element of personality cult in this sort of column: the writer will, over a period of time, build up in his readers' minds an impression of the sort of person he is and of his own style of thinking and living. He will not, therefore, present his views in an impersonal, detached manner.

The nasty sound of youth

I was escorting an old lady along a Kensington pavement last week when three teenaged boys on expensive bicycles rode up behind us hooting their horns impatiently. When I turned on them angrily, they laughed in my face.

Watching this altercation from the steps of their plush house were a middle-aged man and two well-dressed women, to whom I instinctively looked for intimations of moral support. But they seemed to think that it was I who was in the wrong. 'Were you not just as bad when you were their age?' they asked. 'Perhaps so,' I replied, 'but in the event of being caught trying to force an old lady into the gutter, I would have expected to be rebuked.' Needless to say, the three youths were much amused with this exchange and rode off in triumph.

But it left me feeling depressed and baffled. Of course, there have always been young people who lacked consideration for the old. There is nothing new about that. But there is something new – and disturbing – about the willingness of so many adults nowadays to let them get away with it. A world without youthful high spirits would indeed be an unnatural place; but equally unnatural is a world without its fair share of elders prepared to damp them down.

In our street, for example, there is a young gang whose sport it is of an evening to knock over all the neighbourhood dustbins. Nobody seems to protest, in spite of the disgusting mess caused. Some of the parents can even be observed watching with approval. I mentioned this to a social worker friend who has just completed her diploma in sociology. 'Don't you realise,' she retorted, 'that overturning dustbins is just good clean (sic) fun, the contemporary urban equivalent of stealing apples?' — the implication being that these Fulham kids are no worse, say, than Richmal Crompton's hero William.

This may well be so. But surely the point about William's exploits was that they took place against a background of adult disapproval. The curmudgeonly Farmer Jenks waiting to deliver cuffs over the ear was as much an essential part of life in the old days as the naughty boy. Although Richmal Crompton clearly took the view that 'boys will be boys', she was no less clear that adults had an equal right to be adults. The bad temper of the latter was as much a fact of human life as the high spirits of the former.

Today, however, boys are expected to be boys, and to behave accordingly, but adults are not allowed to do likewise. If adults behave naturally, and blow up with rage when provoked beyond endurance, no sociologist comes to their aid with comforting explanations about why it is necessary for them to blow off steam. Although the utmost understanding is lavished on the need for children to be free to express themselves, none is spared on the needs of their elders to give vent to their feelings. It is the old today who are expected to be seen and not heard.

Not so the young. Never in human history has there been so little effort made to make them keep quiet. It is sometimes my fate to travel on the bus or Underground with crowds of children on their way to and from school. The shouting and screaming are indescribable. Yet nobody ever does anything about it, in spite of the fact that noise today, in the cramped conditions of city life, is just as much of a nuisance, just as anti-social, as spitting used to be. Spitting was prohibited because it was unhygienic, a menace to health. So also is making a noise — a menace to mental health. Yet far from being prohibited, it seems to be regarded as an inalienable human right.

Almost every night our street is shaken out of its slumbers in the small hours of the morning by some young motorcyclist roaring through it like a thunderbolt, or by returning revellers slamming their car doors without the slightest concern for the inconvenience caused. People behave in a packed street no less noisily than they would if they were living in some secluded stretch of country, miles away from any other human habitation.

Totally untaught, it seems, is any sense of a code of behaviour suitable to the actual conditions of contemporary city life. Take my own immediate neighbours, for whom in every other respect I have the greatest admiration. On the matter of noise, it seems to me that they are quite literally uncivilised, since they insist on playing pop music very loudly throughout the night. To my complaints they reply that they have a perfect right to do so, on the grounds that they now own the house, having just bought it from the council. An Englishman's home is his castle and so on; so I am told to mind my own business.

But, of course, it is my own business, since the walls that divide their house from mine are paper thin and so far as noise is concerned the two habitations are one, as indeed is the whole street. A code of proprietorial behaviour which made sense in the days when houses stood in their own parks or gardens is utterly unsuited to modern urban living. It is absurd, for example, to see people letting their dogs out onto the city street at night or in the morning with the same carefree abandon as they would if they were living in open country. In these respects, and in so many others, what is required today is a far more rigidly enforced code of social discipline than used to be necessary in former days.

Take litter as another example. In the old days people had much less to throw away. Fewer things were wrapped up. In any case people could afford fewer things. Even the poorest family today probably has more waste to dispose of than used to emerge from a mansion. But no effort is made to train the young into tidy habits. School children can be seen throwing away their packets as if they had individual servants following in their wake to pick the mess up.

In fact this kind of aristocratic disregard for communal sensitivities, which used to be the prerogative of the very few, is now common to all. In the old days it was the upper class which made itself offensive by making too much noise, speaking in those blaring voices that cracked the ear drum. Today all classes feel free to do the same.

The necessity, indeed the virtue, of self-expression — that is the sacred lesson taught in the schools today, not only to the privileged few whose conditions of life may be such as to allow them to put it into practice without hurting others, but also to the great generality of children whose adult lives will be spent in circumstances which require more restraint, more social discipline than ever before, if they are not to make a hell for all. Children running wild in the open country: nothing more natural and idyllic. But not in the modern city, the *nature* of which requires a pedagogic approach based on much more authoritarian values.

Peregrine Worsthorne from 'The Sunday Telegraph'

1   What is the issue in this article? Who is Peregrine Worsthorne condemning? Does he present a new slant on the problem, an original way of considering it?

2   How much of personal reminiscence is there here? What is, for example, the function of the opening couple of paragraphs? What feelings is Worsthorne trying to provoke in the reader by telling this anecdote? What type of reader is he appealing to?

3   How does the writer create the impression that he is a reasonable person living a normal life? Why is it important that he should create such an impression?

4   Analyse the development of thought in this article. What is the main reason for Worsthorne's belief that today we need 'more social discipline than ever before'? At which point in the article does he arrive at this generalisation? What other generalisations does he include?

5   Write your own column, stating your beliefs about some issue which touches school or college life. Try to include relevant material from your own experience (either real or fabricated for the purposes of the article) and build up to a firm conclusion. Avoid stating your main point until you have written enough to ensure that the reader will be on your side and in a state of mind conducive to accepting your point of view.

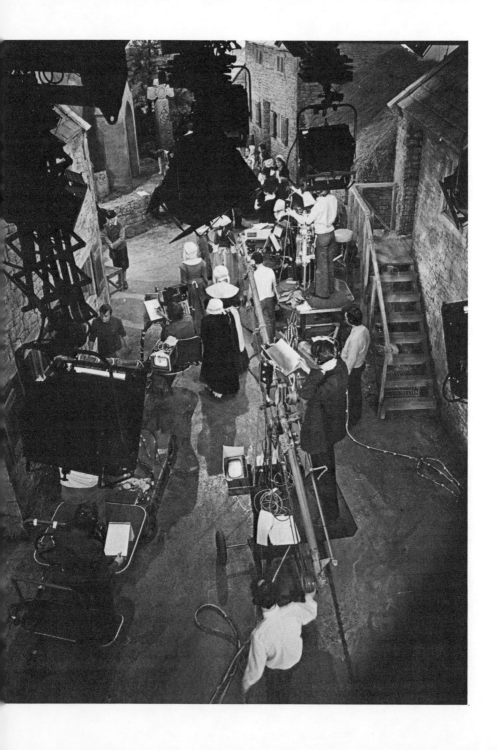

6 Script writing

Stage scripts

What is stage drama? It is easy enough to recognise some of the qualities necessary to an effective play-script, but much more difficult to include them all in a single all embracing definition. We propose, therefore, to approach the subject from a rather different angle: that of adapting a prose narrative (in this case a short story) for the stage – in order to see how much it tells us about the nature of drama in general and the special requirements of play-scripts in particular.

Here first is the prose passage in its original form. It comes from Oscar Wilde's short story *Lord Arthur Savile's Crime*. The background is that, sometime during the late 1890s, Lord Arthur, along with a host of other guests, is attending a grand reception at the fashionable London home of Lady Windermere. At this reception, attention is centred on a certain Mr Septimus Podgers, a chiromantist or palm-reader, who is passing the evening telling the fortunes of those present. When he comes to Lord Arthur, however, Podgers reacts very strangely, looking decidedly uncomfortable and saying that the hand with which he is confronted is nothing more than that 'of a charming young man'. When Arthur and the others present press Podgers to say more, he is clearly reluctant and the situation is only saved for him by the company's decision to go in to supper. Lord Arthur, however, is far from satisfied. He remains beside the fireplace, brooding. . . . .

How mad and monstrous it all seemed! Could it be that written on his hand, in characters that he could not read himself, but that another could decipher, was some fearful secret of sin, some blood-red sign of crime? Was there no escape possible? Were we no better than chessmen, moved by an unseen power, vessels the potter fashions at his fancy, for honour or for shame? His reason revolted against it, and yet he felt that some tragedy was hanging over him, and that he had been suddenly called upon to bear an intolerable burden. Actors are so fortunate. They can choose whether they will appear in tragedy or in comedy, whether they will suffer or make merry, laugh or shed tears. But in real life it is different. Most men and women are forced to perform parts for which they have no qualifications. Our Guildensterns play Hamlet for us, and our Hamlets have to jest like Prince Hal. The world is a stage, but the play is badly cast.

Suddenly Mr Podgers entered the room. When he saw Lord Arthur he started, and his coarse, fat face became a sort of greenish-yellow colour. The two men's eyes met, and for a moment there was silence.

'The Duchess has left one of her gloves here, Lord Arthur, and has asked me to bring it to her,' said Mr Podgers finally. 'Ah, I see it on the sofa! Good evening.'

'Mr Podgers, I must insist on your giving me a straightforward answer to a question I am going to put to you.'

'Another time, Lord Arthur, but the Duchess is anxious. I am afraid I must go.'

'You shall not go. The Duchess is in no hurry.'

'Ladies should not be kept waiting, Lord Arthur,' said Mr Podgers with his sickly smile. 'The fair sex is apt to be impatient.'

Lord Arthur's finely-chiselled lips curled in petulant disdain. The poor Duchess seemed to him of very little importance at that moment. He walked across the room to where Mr Podgers was standing, and held his hand out.

'Tell me what you saw there,' he said. 'Tell me the truth. I must know it. I am not a child.'

Mr Podgers' eyes blinked behind his gold-rimmed spectacles, and he moved uneasily from one foot to the other, while his fingers played nervously with a flash watch-chain.

'What makes you think that I saw anything in your hand, Lord Arthur, more than I told you?'

'I know you did, and I insist on your telling me what it was. I will pay you. I will give you a cheque for a hundred pounds.'

The green eyes flashed for a moment, and then became dull again.

'Guineas?' said Mr Podgers at last, in a low voice.

'Certainly. I will send you a cheque tomorrow. What is your club?'

'I have no club. That is to say, not just at present. My address is——————, but allow me to give you my card'; and producing a bit of gilt-edge pasteboard from his waistcoat pocket, Mr Podgers handed it, with a low bow, to Lord Arthur, who read on it, 'Mr Septimus Podgers, Professional Chiromantist, 1030 West Moon Street.'

'My hours are from ten to four,' murmured Mr Podgers mechanically, 'and I make a reduction for families.'

'Be quick,' cried Lord Arthur, looking very pale, and holding his hand out.

Mr Podgers glanced nervously round, and drew the heavy portière across the door.

'It will take a little time, Lord Arthur, you had better sit down.'

'Be quick, sir,' cried Lord Arthur again, stamping his foot angrily on the polished floor.

Mr Podgers smiled, drew from his breast-pocket a small magnifying glass, and wiped it carefully with his handkerchief.

'I am quite ready,' he said.

Ten minutes later, with face blanched by terror, and eyes wild with grief, Lord Arthur Savile rushed from Bentinck House, crushing his way through the crowd of fur-coated footmen that stood round the large striped awning, and seeming not to see or hear anything. The night was bitter cold, and the gas-lamps round the square flared and flickered in the keen wind; but his hands were hot with fever, and his forehead burned like a fire. On and on he went, almost with the gait of a drunken man. A policeman looked curiously at him as he passed, and a beggar, who slouched from an archway to ask for alms, grew frightened, seeing misery greater than his own. Once he stopped under a lamp, and looked at his hands. He thought he could detect a stain of blood already upon them, and a faint cry broke from his trembling lips.

Murder! that is what the chiromantist had seen there. Murder! The very night seemed to know it, and the desolate wind to howl it in his ear. The dark corners of the streets were full of it. It grinned at him from the roofs of the houses.

from 'Lord Arthur Savile's Crime' by Oscar Wilde

Our next piece is an extract from a musical comedy by Richard Adams based on Wilde's short story and entitled *It's a Crime!!* In his version, Richard Adams departs quite radically from the original both in matters of detail and in general tone. But what concerns us chiefly is the fact that in making his adaptation, Adams was obliged to keep in mind the special requirements of writing for the stage. Before considering – in an episode from *It's a Crime!!* which corresponds exactly with the passage from *Lord Arthur Savile's Crime* you have just read – how well or otherwise the adapter has coped with his task, look back at Wilde's original and think how you might deal with the same problem yourself. Here are some questions to help focus your thoughts:

1   The revelation of Lord Arthur's destiny to murder is made by Wilde at the end of one and the beginning of a second chapter in his story. Could this device be possibly made to work on the stage? Does the change of scenes present problems?

2   There is a crucial (and very effective) omission in Wilde's account. Can you identify it? How would you fill this gap (if at all) in a stage version of the episode?

3   Which aspects of Wilde's narrative would be (a) impossible to translate into stage terms; (b) possible on the stage but awkward; (c) both possible and convincing?

4   Which of Lord Arthur's and Podgers's words could be retained without alteration? Which could be kept, though with some modification? Which would need to be omitted entirely? Is there anything that needs to be added which Wilde has not included?

5   Some of Wilde's description of the manner adopted by the two men in this scene could well be used as stage directions and guides to interpretation in a play-script. Which lines might well be used in this way? Which would be best ignored? Is there any danger in sticking to the original too slavishly when it comes to making this sort of adaptation?

Here now is the extract from *It's a Crime!!*:

(*Enter* PODGERS *smiling conspiratorially pursued by an agitated* LORD ARTHUR)

LORD ARTHUR: Stop!! I say, stop, Mr Podgers! (PODGERS *turns and waits*) You just can't leave me like that!

PODGERS: My dear sir, like what?

LORD ARTHUR: Like without telling me what it was you saw in my palm.

PODGERS: But, forgive me, I *did* tell you.

LORD ARTHUR: Pah! D'you really think I'm satisfied with that? Not content with positively avoiding me in there (*points into the other room*), all you could say when I *did* manage to stick my hand in front of your nose was that 'this is the hand —

PODGERS: — of a charming young man.' Yes. Well, what of it? What do you want me to say?

LORD ARTHUR: My *future* — that's what I want to hear about. You told all the others what lies in store for them. So what about me? You're concealing something from me, I know it. You can't hoodwink me, you know; I'm not a child! (PODGERS *gives a disdainful look and makes as if to leave*) (LORD ARTHUR *tries a new tack*) I'll — I'll pay you! I'll give you a hundred pounds — (*reaching to find his wallet*)

PODGERS: (*quietly, with new interest*) Guineas?

LORD ARTHUR: I'll send you a cheque in the morning!

PODGERS: (*looking at him icily*) Very well. Pray be seated, Lord Arthur. It may take a little time. (*glances furtively round the room*) (*They sit.* PODGERS *takes out a large magnifying-glass and wipes it methodically*)

LORD ARTHUR: Oh do be quick!

PODGERS: (*examining hand*) Yes, well — all in good time . . . all in good time — mmm. I see . . . I see you taking a journey, a voyage — perhaps a long voyage — in the next few months.

LORD ARTHUR: My honeymoon! (*impatient*) Yes, yes, go on!

PODGERS: No — not your honeymoon. Another journey — of a quite different nature. Yes. (*Looks closer*) Yes . . . and you will soon lose (*looks slyly at* LORD ARTHUR) a relative. A relative of yours will die.

LORD ARTHUR: A relative! But who? No one close, I hope.

PODGERS: On the contrary, no one of any real consequence. A distant relative merely. (*again the slow scrutiny — then, horrorstruck, he drops the hand*) And that is all! (*he rises*)

LORD ARTHUR: All? It can't be all! Why have you stopped? What about my marriage? What about Miss Merton?

PODGERS: (*cold*) What about them indeed? They are nothing to me.

LORD ARTHUR: (*seizes* PODGERS) There *was* something, wasn't there?! Tell me! I demand it!

PODGERS: (*releases himself with dignity*) Very well. If you insist. I *did* see your marriage and I *did* see Miss Merton, but neither seems destined to feature in the foreground of your future. They are obscured by another event. One much closer.

LORD ARTHUR: Well?

PODGERS: A crime.

LORD ARTHUR: Crime?

PODGERS: Yes. To be precise, a murder. You, Lord Arthur Savile, are shortly to commit a murder! (*exit with a flourish*)

   from 'It's a Crime!!', words by Richard Adams, music by Robin Nelson

1   In what ways has Richard Adams changed the mood of the original? How is this reflected especially in Podgers's manner?

2   In what ways has the feeling of tension and expectation been maintained?

3   Bearing in mind the conclusions you will have come to about how you might perform a similar exercise, consider how successfully Adams has adapted this moment from *Lord Arthur Savile's Crime* for a musical comedy.

4   What particular qualities of climax, change of mood and pace, and characterisation, are there evident in the passage from *It's a Crime!!*?

5   Choose a passage from one of your favourite novels or short stories (preferably one containing a certain amount of dialogue) and try your hand at adapting it for the stage. Prepare your play-script in detail, including stage-directions, and get a group of your friends to read and act it through to see how well it sounds and looks.

Dramatic intensity

The three extracts in this section have been chosen to give you a glimpse of the great range of effect that dramatists have achieved in the theatre. In one way or another most playwrights attempt to achieve an intensity, a focussing of the audience's feelings: laughter or tears, tension or anxiety are wrought up to a pitch as we watch the enactment of feelings which in everyday life tend to be muted or dissipated by more humdrum concerns.

The first extract, from Edward Albee's *Who's Afraid of Virginia Woolf?*, presents four characters, two married couples who have just met at a party in a small American college. They have all been drinking heavily and Martha and George – the middle-aged couple – have invited Honey and Nick – a younger couple, new to the campus – back to their house for a night-cap. Martha's father is president of the college and when this extract begins, she is telling Nick about how she came to marry George.

MARTHA: And I got the idea, about then, that I'd marry into the college . . . which didn't seem to be quite as stupid as it turned out. I mean, Daddy had a sense of history . . . of . . . continuation . . . Why don't you come over here and sit by me?

NICK (*indicating* HONEY, *who is barely with it*): I . . . don't think I . . . should . . . I . . .

MARTHA: Suit yourself. A sense of continuation . . . history . . . and he'd always had it in the back of his mind to . . . *groom* someone to take over . . . some time, when he quit. A succession . . . you know what I mean?

NICK: Yes, I do.

MARTHA: Which is natural enough. When you've made something, you want to pass it on, to somebody. So, I was sort of on the lookout, for, . . . prospects with the new men. An heir-apparent. (*Laughs*) It wasn't *Daddy's* idea that I had to necessarily marry the guy. I mean, I wasn't the albatross . . . you didn't have to take me to get the prize, or anything like that. It was something *I* had in the back of *my* mind. And a lot of the new men were married . . . naturally.

NICK: Sure.

MARTHA: (*with a strange smile*): Like you, baby.

HONEY (*a mindless echo*): Like you, baby.

MARTHA (*ironically*): But then George came along . . . along came George.

GEORGE (*re-entering, with liquor*): And along came George, bearing hooch. What are you doing now, Martha?

MARTHA (*unfazed*): I'm telling a story. Sit down . . . . you'll learn something.

GEORGE (*stays standing. Puts the liquor on the portable bar*): All rightie.

HONEY: You've come back!

GEORGE: That's right.

HONEY: Dear! He's come back!

NICK: Yes, I see . . . I see.

MARTHA: Where was I?

HONEY: I'm *so* glad.

NICK: Shhhh.

HONEY (*imitating him*): Shhhh.

MARTHA: Oh yeah. And along came George. That's right. WHO was young . . . intelligent . . . and . . . bushy-tailed, and . . . sort of cute . . . if you can imagine it . . .

GEORGE: . . . and younger than you . . .

MARTHA: . . . and younger than me . . .

GEORGE: . . . by six years . . .

MARTHA: . . . by six years . . . It doesn't bother me, George . . . And along he came, bright-eyed, into the History Department. And you know what I did, dumb cluck that I am? You know what I did? I fell for him.

HONEY (*dreamy*): Oh, that's nice.

GEORGE: Yes, she did. You should have seen it. She'd sit outside of my room, on the lawn, at night, and she'd howl and claw at the turf . . . I couldn't work.

MARTHA (*laughs, really amused*): I actually fell for him . . . it . . . that, there.

GEORGE: Martha's a Romantic at heart.

MARTHA: That I am. So, I actually fell for him. And the match seemed . . . practical, too. You know, Daddy was looking for someone to . . .

GEORGE: Just a minute, Martha . . .

MARTHA: . . . take over, some time, when he was ready to . . .

GEORGE (*stony*): Just a minute, Martha.

MARTHA: . . . retire, and so I thought . . .

GEORGE: STOP IT, MARTHA!

MARTHA(*irritated*): Whadda you want?

GEORGE(*too patiently*): I'd thought you were telling the story of our courtship, Martha . . . I didn't know you were going to start in on the other business.

MARTHA: (*so-thereish*): Well, I am!

GEORGE: I wouldn't, if I were you.

MARTHA: Oh, . . .you wouldn't? Well, you're not!

GEORGE: Now, you've already sprung a leak about you-know-what . . .

MARTHA (*a duck*): What? What?

GEORGE: . . . about the apple of our eye . . . the sprout . . . the little bugger . . .(*spits it out*) . . . our *son* . . . and if you start on this other business, I warn you, Martha, it's going to make me angry.

MARTHA (*laughing at him*): Oh, it is, is it?

GEORGE: I warn you.

MARTHA (*incredulous*): You *what*?

GEORGE (*very quietly*): I warn you.

NICK: Do you really think we have to go through . . . ?

MARTHA: I stand warned! (*Pause . . . then, to* HONEY *and* NICK) So, anyway, I married the S.O.B. and I had it all planned out . . . He was the groom . . . he was going to be groomed. He'd take over some day . . . first, he'd take over the History Department, and then, when Daddy retired, he'd take over the college . . . you know? That's the way it was supposed to be. (*to* GEORGE, *who is at the portable bar with his back to her*)

You getting angry, baby? Hunh? (*now back*) That's the way it was *supposed* to be. Very simple. And Daddy seemed to think it was a pretty good idea, too. For a while. Until he watched for a couple of years! (*To* GEORGE *again*) You getting angrier? (*Now back*) Until he watched for a couple of years and started thinking maybe it wasn't such a good idea after all . . . that maybe Georgie-boy didn't have the stuff . . . that he didn't have it in him!

GEORGE (*still with his back to them all*): Stop it, Martha.

MARTHA (*viciously triumphant*): The hell I will! You see, George didn't have much . . . push . . . he wasn't particularly aggressive. In fact he was sort of a . . . (*Spits the word at* GEORGE's *back*): . . . a FLOP! A great . . . big . . . flat . . . FLOP!

(CRASH! *Immediately after* FLOP! GEORGE *breaks a bottle against the portable bar and stands there, still with his back to them all, holding the remains of the bottle by the neck. There is a silence, with everyone frozen. Then . . .*)

GEORGE (*almost crying*): I said stop, Martha.

MARTHA (*after considering what course to take*): I hope that was an empty bottle, George. You don't want to waste good liquor . . . not on your salary.

(GEORGE *drops the broken bottle on the floor, not moving*) Not on an Associate Professor's salary. (*To* NICK *and* HONEY) I mean, he'd be . . . no good . . . at trustees' dinners, fund raising. He didn't have any . . . personality, you know what I mean? Which was disappointing to Daddy, as you can imagine. So, here I am, stuck with this flop . . .

GEORGE (*turning round*): . . . don't go on, Martha . . .

MARTHA: . . . this BOG in the History Department . . .

GEORGE: . . . don't Martha, don't . . .

MARTHA (*her voice rising to match his*) . . . who's married to the President's daughter, who's expected to *be* somebody, not just some nobody, some bookworm, somebody who's so damn . . . contemplative, he can't make anything out of himself, somebody without the *guts* to make anybody proud of him . . . ALL RIGHT, GEORGE!

GEORGE (*under her, then covering, to drown her*): I said, don't. All right . . . all right: (*sings*) Who's afraid of Virginia Woolf, Virginia Woolf, Virginia Woolf, Who's afraid of Virginia Woolf, early in the morning.

GEORGE and HONEY (*who joins him drunkenly*):
Who's afraid of Virginia Woolf,
Virginia Woolf,
Virginia Woolf . . . (*etc.*)

MARTHA: STOP IT!

(*a brief silence*)

HONEY (*rising, moving towards the hall*): I'm going to be sick . . . I'm going to be sick . . . I'm goint to vomit. (*Exits*)

NICK (*going after her*): Oh, for God's sake! (*Exits*)

MARTHA (*going after them, looks back at* GEORGE *contemptuously*): Jesus! (*Exits.* GEORGE *is alone on stage.*)

Curtain

from '*Who's Afraid of Virginia Woolf?*' by Edward Albee

1   What is revealed to the audience in this extract about the relationship between George and Martha? How would you describe their personalities? How do they treat each other? What feelings would this interaction provoke in the audience?

2   Why do you think there are so many directions as to the manner in which this dialogue is to be spoken? Listen to a couple of readings of

the scene done by members of your class and try to get a clear sense of the manner in which the dialogue is to be spoken.

3 Examine the roles of Nick and Honey in this scene. Is it essential that they be present or could the same effect of tension be achieved without them?

4 What actions contribute to the build-up of tension as Martha's story unfolds?

5 This extract is taken from the first act of a three act play. How do you imagine the rest of the play might proceed, supposing — as is, in fact, the case — that no further characters are introduced and that these four people remain in the same place for the next couple of hours and continue to drink steadily?

The second extract constitutes the final moments of a short, tragic play set on a remote island off the West of Ireland. Maurya is an old peasant woman who has lost her husband, her father-in-law and all but one of her six sons in various drowning accidents. The play concerns her premonition that Bartley, her last son, is also to be lost at sea. Nora and Cathleen are her daughters.

CATHLEEN (*begins to keen*): It's destroyed we are from this day. It's destroyed, surely.

NORA: Didn't the young priest say the Almighty God won't leave her destitute with no son living?

MAURYA (*in a low voice, but clearly*): It's little the like of him knows of the sea . . . Bartley will be lost now, and let you call in Eamon and make me a good coffin out of the white boards, for I won't live after them. I've had a husband, and a husband's father, and six sons in this house — six fine men, though it was a hard birth I had with every one of them and they coming into the world — and some of them were found and some of them were not found, but they're gone now the lot of them . . . There were Stephen, and Shawn, were lost in the great wind, and found after in the Bay of Gregory of the Golden Mouth, and carried up the two of them on one plank, and in by that door.

(*She pauses for a moment: the girls start as if they heard something through the door that is half open behind them.*)

NORA (*in a whisper*): Did you hear that, Cathleen? Did you hear a noise in the north-east?

CATHLEEN (*in a whisper*): There's someone after crying out by the seashore.

MAURYA (*continues without hearing anything*): There was Sheamus and his father, and his own father again, were lost in a dark night, and not a stick or sign was seen of them when the sun went up. There was Patch after was drowned out of a curagh that turned over. I was sitting here with Bartley, and he a baby, lying on my two knees, and I seen two women, and three women, and four women coming in, and they crossing themselves, and not saying a word. I looked out then, and there were men coming after them, and they holding a thing in the half of a red sail, and water dripping out of it — it was a dry day, Nora — and leaving a track to the door.

(*She pauses again with her hand stretched out towards the door. It opens softly and old women begin to come in, crossing themselves on the threshold, and kneeling down in front of the stage with red petticoats over their heads.*)

MAURYA (*half in a dream, to* CATHLEEN): Is it Patch, or Michael, or what is it at all?

CATHLEEN: Michael is after being found in the far north, and when he is found there how could he be here in this place?

MAURYA: There does be a power of young men floating round in the sea, and what way would they know if it was Michael they had, or another man like him, for when a man is nine days in the sea, and the wind blowing, it's hard set his own mother would be to say what man was in it.

CATHLEEN: It's Michael. God spare him, for they're after sending us a bit of his clothes from the far north.

(*She reaches out and hands* MAURYA *the clothes that belonged to Michael.* MAURYA *stands up slowly, and takes them in her hands.* NORA *looks out.*)

NORA: They're carrying a thing among them and there's water dripping out of it and leaving a track by the big stones.

CATHLEEN (*in a whisper to the women who have come in*): Is it Bartley it is?

ONE OF THE WOMEN: It is surely, God rest his soul.

(*Two younger women come in and pull out the table. Then men carry in the body of* BARTLEY, *laid on a plank, with a bit of sail over it, and lay it on the table.*)

CATHLEEN (*to the women as they are doing so.*): What way was he drowned?

ONE OF THE WOMEN: The grey pony knocked him over into the sea, and he was washed out where there is a great surf on the white rocks.

(MAURYA *has gone over and knelt down at the head of the table. The women are keening softly and swaying themselves with a slow movement.* CATHLEEN *and* NORA *kneel at the other end of the table. The men kneel near the door.*)

MAURYA (*raising her head and speaking as if she did not see the people around her*): They're all gone now, and there isn't anything more the sea can do to me . . . . I'll have no call now to be up crying and praying when the wind breaks from the south, and you can hear the surf is in the east, and the surf is in the west making a great stir with the two noises, and they hitting one on the other. I'll have no call now to be going down and getting Holy Water in the dark nights after Samhain, and I won't care what way the sea is when the other women will be keening. (*To* NORA) Give me the Holy Water, Nora, there's a small sup still on the dresser. (NORA *gives it to her.* MAURYA *drops Michael's clothes across* BARTLEY's *feet and sprinkles the Holy Water over him*) . . . It isn't that I haven't prayed for you, Bartley, to the Almighty God. It isn't that I haven't said prayers in the dark night till you wouldn't know what I'd be saying; but it's a great rest I'll have now, and it's time surely. It's a great rest I'll have now, and great sleeping in the long nights after Samhain, if it's only a bit of wet flour we do have to eat, and maybe a fish that would be stinking. (*She kneels down again, crossing herself, and saying prayers under her breath.*)

CATHLEEN (*to an old man kneeling near her*): Maybe yourself and Eamon would make a coffin when the sun rises. We have fine white boards herself bought, God help her, thinking Michael would be found, and I have a new cake you can eat while you'll be working.

THE OLD MAN (*looking at the boards*): Are there nails with them?

CATHLEEN: There are not, Colum; we didn't think of the nails.

ANOTHER MAN: It's a great wonder she wouldn't think of the nails, and all the coffins she's seen made already.

CATHLEEN: It's getting old she is, and broken.

(MAURYA *stands up again very slowly and spreads out the pieces of Michael's clothes beside the body, sprinkling them with the last of the Holy Water.*)

NORA (*in a whisper to* CATHLEEN): She's quiet now and easy; but the day Michael was drowned you could hear her crying out from this to the spring well. It's fonder she was of Michael, and would any one have thought that?

CATHLEEN (*slowly and clearly*): An old woman will soon be tired with anything she will do, and isn't it nine days herself is after crying, and keening, and making great sorrow in the house?

MAURYA (*puts the empty cup mouth downwards on the table, and lays her hands together on* BARTLEY'*s feet.*): They're all together this time, and the end is come. May the Almighty God have mercy on Bartley's soul, and on Michael's soul, and on the souls of Sheamus and Patch, and Stephen and Shawn (*bending her head*) . . . . and may He have mercy on my soul, Nora, and on the soul of everyone is left living in the world. (*She pauses, and the keen rises a little more loudly from the women, then sinks away. Continuing.*) Michael has a clean burial in the far north, by the grace of the Almighty God. Bartley will have a fine coffin out of the white boards, and a deep grave surely . . . . What more can we want than that? . . . . No man at all can be living for ever, and we must be satisfied.

(*She kneels down again and the curtain falls slowly.*)
The End
 from 'Riders to the Sea' by J. H. Synge

1 Sadness and pathos are obviously the feelings likely to be produced by the overwhelming tragedy of this play. By what means are these feelings intensified through this extract? Consider the appropriateness of the moment of entry of the women and of Bartley's body. Consider the importance of ritualised action in the scene, the effect of the sudden crowding of the scene and of the women's keening.

2 Examine the comments made by Nora and Cathleen. How do they contribute to the overall impact of the scene?

3 Discuss Maurya's speeches. How would you describe her attitude to these events? What is her philosophy of life? Take into account her comments on the words of the young priest and especially her final speech. To what extent does she seem like an ordinary woman, an

individual, and to what extent does she emerge as representative of universal and enduring human qualities?

4 Sum up the details in this scene that help to keep it 'real' and related to everyday life and then try to sum up all that lifts it beyond everyday experience.

Macbeth is a play about ambition and about the disintegration of strong personalities once they have succumbed to pursuing their ambition by evil means. Macbeth has murdered Duncan, the king of Scotland, and replaced him on the throne. Lady Macbeth has goaded him on. Now, safely crowned, neither of them feels safe and Macbeth has made arrangements for Banquo, who suspects him, to be murdered. This short scene occurs between the coronation of Macbeth and a banquet to celebrate the event.

(*Enter* LADY MACBETH *and a Servant*)
LADY MACBETH: Is Banquo gone from court?
SERVANT: Ay, madam, but returns again tonight.
LADY MACBETH: Say to the king, I would attend his leisure
    For a few words.
SERVANT: Madam, I will.   (*Exit*)
LADY MACBETH: Nought's had, all's spent,
    Where our desire is got without content: 5
    'Tis safer to be that which we destroy
    Than by destruction dwell in doubtful joy,
    (*Enter* MACBETH)
    How now, my lord! why do you keep alone,
    Of sorriest fancies your companions making,
    Using those thoughts which should indeed have died   10
    With them they think on? Things without all remedy
    Should be without regard: what's done is done.
MACBETH: We have scotch'd the snake, not kill'd it:
    She'll close and be herself, whilst our poor malice
    Remains in danger of her former tooth.   15

7 *by destruction*: by destroying someone else. 13 *scotch'd*: cut, gashed, 15 *former tooth*: the tooth she had before the 'scotching' and still has.

But let the frame of things disjoint, both the worlds suffer,
Ere we will eat our meal in fear, and sleep
In the affliction of these terrible dreams
That shake us nightly. Better be with the dead,
Whom we, to gain our peace, have sent to peace,   20
Than on the torture of the mind to lie
In restless ecstasy. Duncan is in his grave;
After life's fitful fever he sleeps well;
Treason has done his worst: nor steel, nor poison,
Malice domestic, foreign levy, nothing   25
Can touch him further.

LADY MACBETH: Come on;
Gentle my lord, sleek o'er your rugged looks;
Be bright and jovial among your guests to-night.

MACBETH: So shall I, love; and so, I pray, be you.
Let your remembrance apply to Banquo;   30
Present him eminence, both with eye and tongue:
Unsafe the while, that we
Must lave our honours in these flattering streams,
And make our faces vizards to our hearts,
Disguising what they are.

LADY MACBETH: You must leave this.   35

MACBETH: O! full of scorpions is my mind, dear wife;
Thou know'st that Banquo and his Fleance lives.

LADY MACBETH: But in them nature's copy's not eterne.

MACBETH: There's comfort yet; they are assailable;
Then be thou jocund. Ere the bat hath flown   40
His cloister'd flight, ere to black Hecate's summons
The shard-born beetle with his drowsy hums
Hath rung night's yawning peal, there shall be done
A deed of dreadful note.

LADY MACBETH: What's to be done?

---

16 *the frame of things*: the universe; *disjoint*: fall asunder. *both the worlds*: heaven and earth. 22 *ecstacy*: the state of being 'beside oneself'. 24 *his*: its. 27 *sleek o'er*: smooth down (like hair). 30 *apply to*: be given to. 31 *Present him eminence*: pay him special honour. 34 *vizards*: masks. 38 *copy*: copyhold or lease. Nature has not given them an eternal lease of life. 41 *cloister'd*: among cloisters. 42 *shard-born*: born in dung. 43 *yawning peal*: the peal which invites to slumber.

MACBETH: Be innocent of the knowledge, dearest chuck, 45
Till thou applaud the deed. Come, seeling night,
Scarf up the tender eye of pitiful day,
And with thy bloody and invisible hand
Cancel and tear to pieces that great bond
Which keeps me pale! Light thickens, and the crow 50
Makes wing to the rooky wood;
Good things of day begin to droop and drowse,
Whiles night's black agents to their preys do rouse.
Thou marvell'st at my words: but hold thee still;
Things bad begun make strong themselves by ill: 55
So, prithee, go with me.   (*Exeunt*)
    from 'Macbeth' by William Shakespeare, ed. B. Groom

1   What insights are we given into the state of mind of Lady
Macbeth and of Macbeth himself and what can you deduce about their
present relationship?

2   Consider the content of the two speeches of Macbeth which bring
this short scene to a close. How does Shakespeare create an atmosphere
of intense evil through them? Consider too the extent to which you are
aware of a questioning of what is good and what is evil throughout the
scene.

3   In this scene, as in the whole play, we sense that there are forces
urging the action forward. These forces are not located simply in the
ambitious desires of the two chief characters: Shakespeare universalises
them so that Macbeth and Lady Macbeth are victims of powers of evil
greater than they can control. By what means are we made aware of the
power of evil in this scene?

4   In looking again over these three extracts, try to distinguish the
different sorts of intensity that are created in each one. Which would you
call the most 'atmospheric' scene, the most 'moving'? Which depends
most for its effect on intense interaction between the characters? What
other sorts of dramatic intensity have you experienced in the theatre?

For improvisation and writing

1   In groups, discuss a family situation that builds up to a violent row
and then improvise the scene in such a way as to create a crescendo of

46 *seeling*: blinding.   49 *bond*: the bond by which Banquo and Fleance hold their lives
from Nature.

intense interaction between the characters. Write out a script of the scene.

2   Conceive of a scene in which the rituals of a marriage or a funeral, or a courtroom or a state occasion dominate the action. Improvise it and write up the scene paying particular attention to the stage directions.

3   Try writing a scene to be performed on a bare stage in the open air without sound effects. Conceive of a situation taking place at night or during a violent thunderstorm and try to convey the atmosphere through the language you use.

Film scripts

In most cases it is easier to adapt prose for the screen than it is to adapt it for the stage. As we have already seen in the opening section of this unit, the playwright is restricted in ways that the prose writer is not. The film script-writer, on the other hand, because he is able to switch either the viewpoint or the setting as frequently as he wishes, has a much wider variety of options open to him.

The following extract is taken from a film script by Dylan Thomas, which is an adaptation of *Twenty Years A-Growing*, the autobiography of the Irish writer Maurice O'Sullivan. The book tells the story of O'Sullivan's childhood on the lonely Blasket Islands, which lie off the Kerry coast in the extreme south-western corner of Ireland.

Dissolve to:
(*The interior of Maurice's cottage. Close, we see a table piled with apples and oranges and sweets and cakes and tarts, and we hear voices and the laughter of young girls, and the noise of the wind outside.*

We **track back** *to see the whole room; the lamps alight, a great peat fire burning, the ticking clock.*

Maurice's sisters, Maura and Eileen, are busy at the hearth and over the pots on the fire. Mauraid is scattering white sand on the floor. Other girls are washing plates and setting knives and forks on the table. And we hear:)
THE VOICE: Praise to God for His gifts,
   for a roof and a fire,
   a red red fire in the cold winter night
   in a house on the edge of the seas.
   And the wind be wild and the house do be bright . . .

and the girls do be busy as bees . . .
Winter had come to the island, and Halloween
was upon us, and outside in the blowing dark
the boys were hunting thrushes.

*(And we are outside the house now, on the wild island; the island
thrown up black against the phosphorous sea.*

We see the bobbing pinpoints of lanterns on the stormy cliffs.

*Now we are closer to the cliffs. Three lanterns bob towards us, and
then stop. In their light we see the faces of Maurice and Tomas and a
youth, Padrig Peg . . .*

Padrig lifts his hand out of his oilskin pocket.

*We see the hand close, in the lantern light. It is full of dead
thrushes.)*

PADRIG: Six.

(Tomas puts out his hand.)

TOMAS: Three here.

(Maurice puts out his hand.)

MAURICE: One. I had my hands around two more but they pecked
me like puffins.

(A bird's cry — giog-giog-giog — comes out of the darkness.)

MAURICE *(whispering)*: What is that?

PADRIG: It is a peewit . . . It's blinded in the light . . . What did
you think it was . . . ?

*(Padrig thrusts his hand into a sparse and wind-blown bush and pulls
out the bird still crying. The crying stops.)*

PADRIG: Now we will go down Seal Cove . . . Quiet! Dead quiet!
Take it fine and easy. Don't be afraid.

Cut:

*(Now we see, from the cliff edge, the three lanterns bobbing down the
cliff. The noise of the sea shouts up to us. Blackness, and the three bobbing
lights. Blackness, and the hollow shouting of the sea.*

Cut:

*Now we are close to the three boys standing in the cove. They move
their lanterns slowly in half-circles, illuminating the great rocks and the
sea breaking upon them, and we hear:)*

THE VOICE *(softly)*: You would think the living and the dead were
there with the roar of the waves and the hiss of foam . . .

PADRIG: Don't be afraid. And don't speak a word till we get across
to the patch of soil there. The thrushes are all sleeping now . . .

(*Now we see the lanterns bobbing across the cove, and across the crevice and the patch of soil.*

Close, we see Padrig thrust his hand into the crevice and draw out a thrush. And again. And again. And again. As he is capturing the sleeping birds, so Maurice and Tomas, moving their lanterns to light the battering sea, speak fearfully:)

TOMAS: Are you afraid at all?

MAURICE: The devil a bit . . .

TOMAS: It's often my father told me that people had been heard speaking here . . .

MAURICE: Oh, whisht, Tomas, do not say that . . .

TOMAS: But they were not people indeed.

MAURICE: Faith, it is I know they were not . . .

(*Now from another part of the cove we see the wavering lanterns, we see mighty waves roaring in and crashing on the rocks.*

Now the three lanterns' lights move up the cliff.

Now from the edge of the cliff we look down on to the three lights climbing up towards us. They come closer. We see, in the lantern light, the three boys scrambling up and clinging on to one another's coat tails.

Now the light is blindingly near us.

And now we are back in the bright cottage, at the end of the room farthest from the door. It is full of boys and girls. The girls are beginning to pluck the sparrows heaped on a table.

The door is flung open. The wind hurling in, and then Maurice and Tomas and Padrig, spindrift-wet and wild-haired.

There is a noise in the house, of the voices of children merry together, and a boy calls out, and this cry is taken up by other voices, as the three enter.)

A BOY: How many have you?

ANOTHER BOY: How many now . . . ?

ANOTHER BOY: Oh, look at them all . . .

A BOY: I got twenty . . .

PADRIG: Faith, we have twenty-eight . . .

(*The three throw their thrushes on to a table . . .*

Cut to:

The thrushes roasting on the fire. We hear the music of a melodeon.

Pan along *the room slowly from the fire.*

A young man is sitting on the floor, back against the wall, playing the melodeon.

Four girls and four boys are dancing a set, which is a dance like the old quadrille.

Boys and girls are sitting at the table, eating. Some stand, eating the little roasted birds with their fingers, watching the dancing.

A girl is sitting on a boy's knee.

Boys are leaping up at a big apple hung by a rope from the rafters, trying to take bites out of it.

Now we are close to a tub of water and a little group of boys and girls, Mauraid and Maurice among them, kneeling around it.

A boy and a girl, at the same time, throw a bean each into the water.)

MAURAID (*softly, looking at Maurice*): If the bean sink in the water, it is a sign that Michael and Brigid do love one another . . .

THE GIRL BRIGID: Och, they are floating . . .

(*Mauraid puts a bean in Maurice's hand.*)

MAURAID: Will you try?

(*Maurice throws a bean into the water, and, as he does so, Mauraid throws one in also.*

We see the beans sink in the water . . .

Now we see close the faces of Mauraid and Maurice.

And now nearly all the boys and girls are dancing. The melodeon is playing a gay tune. Maurice is dancing with Mauraid . . . the music rises.)

Fade out

from 'Twenty Years A-Growing' by Dylan Thomas

1 What aspects of life on the Blasket Islands is Dylan Thomas seeking to convey in these scenes?

2 How frequently is the setting changed? What effects do the changes of setting achieve?

3 Who is '*The Voice*'? Discuss what he says and why Dylan Thomas introduces his comments in the places where they occur.

4 How does Dylan Thomas create the atmosphere of the scene on the cliffs? Discuss his use of different camera shots, of sounds and of dialogue.

5 What is the mood of the people inside the cottage? How does Dylan Thomas convey their mood to the audience?

6 Dylan Thomas specifies the music that can be heard inside the cottage and some of the sounds that can be heard on the cliffs. If you were directing the film of the scenes what other music or sounds, if any,

would you include on the soundtrack to accompany the pictures of the scene on the cliffs?

7   Choose a section from an autobiography, such as Laurie Lee's *Cider with Rosie*, James Kirkup's *The Only Child* or Gavin Maxwell's *Ring of Bright Water* and write a film script based on it.

Television scripts

Often the changes of setting or viewpoint in a film or television script are more frequent and more varied than in Dylan Thomas's script. Here is a short section from the early part of a television play, *Speech Day*, by Barry Hines, the author of *Kes*.

(*Interior boys' bedroom*
A medium shot of Ronnie still asleep.
Cut to
Exterior flats.
A long shot of Ronnie on his way to school.
Interior factory.
We see a steel furnace. A truck is coming from furnace pulling out and moving away.
Close-up of a man drinking tea with Mr Warboys who is reading a paper.)
MR. WARBOYS: What about this two pound limit on rises then, Joe?
(**Cut to** *a long shot of the school buildings. We hear the Headmaster's voice. Then we move into the school hall, and see him on the platform.*)
HEADMASTER: The timetable will be as normal this morning. Will all pupils who are receiving prizes this afternoon meet in the hall for a short while directly after break this morning? The Speech Day Ceremony will commence at two o'clock. Stay in your own form rooms after the afternoon registration and each form will be sent for individually.
(*Outside the school.*
Miss Bedford is just getting out of her car and closing the door. She turns as Ronnie comes up.)
MISS BEDFORD: Good morning, Ronnie.
RONNIE: Late again, Miss.
MISS BEDFORD: You can talk, lad.
RONNIE: Five minutes late. You'd have time stopped at our Danny's place for that.
MISS BEDFORD: Time stopped?

RONNIE: Yeh. They allow 'em three minutes a week. Anything over that they knock 'em half an hour's pay off.

(*The factory.*

We see Danny and an old man finishing drinking tea, throwing away the paper cups and going off.

The school hall.)

HEADMASTER: I do not have to tell you, of course, that important guests will be in school this afternoon. You will be under public scrutiny. Your conduct will be impeccable, your appearance immaculate, which means, of course, full school uniform. That is all. Dismiss.

(*We see the pupils beginning to leave and the Headmaster watching them.*

Outside the hall.

The Headmaster comes out, down the steps to look around. He sees some litter and goes back in. In the classroom Ronnie, Wally and other boys are seen playing 'Hands'. The Headmaster walks along the corridor to a notice board on the wall. He runs his finger along the board.

The Headmaster's study.

The Headmaster is looking out of the window, talking to Mr Clarkson.)

HEADMASTER: I'm a little concerned about the school grounds, Mr Clarkson. I thought it might look a shade tidier.

MR CLARKSON: Do you want me to ask George to see to it?

(*A classroom.*

Ronnie and the others are settling down. Miss Bedford is handing out books.)

MISS BEDFORD: Right boys, I'm going to give you a treat today.

(*The boys start to laugh and hum 'The Stripper' miming the actions.*

The Headmaster's study.)

HEADMASTER: Could you please see to those arrangements, Mr Clarkson?

MR CLARKSON: Would you mind if I asked Mr Douglas to attend to it Headmaster? I really am up to the neck, what with one thing and another.

HEADMASTER: Certainly. Let's have all the senior staff pulling their weight. After all, that's what we're paid extra for.

(*The classroom.*)

MISS BEDFORD: Soccer and sex, that's all you think about.

WALLY: We never said a word, Miss.

MISS BEDFORD: You didn't have to, did you? Now look after these books, lads. They've just arrived and you're the first class in the

being an Officer isn't enough.

school to use them. In my opinion this is one of the best sets of stories around today.

JOHN: The best books for the best class, eh Miss?

MISS BEDFORD: That's right, John. (*She sits on the desk and opens the book.*) Now I'll just tell you something about the author before we begin. (*She notices a boy yawning.*) Come on, Martin, now don't say you're bored. We haven't even started yet.

MARTIN: I'm not, Miss. I'm just tired that's all.

JOHN: There's no wonder. He's out with his bird every night.

from 'Speech Day' by Barry Hines

1 Discuss how often the scene changes in this short section of script. Why are there so many changes? What is the purpose of each one?

2 Discuss the various pieces of dialogue and explain what Barry Hines is aiming to convey to the audience through each one.

3 What impression have you gained from these scenes of (a) Ronnie (b) Miss Bedford (c) the Headmaster? How has Barry Hines conveyed these impressions to you?

4 Write a television script of your own about an important day in someone's life. Experiment with varying the viewpoint, so that you show the incidents that occur from a number of different angles and not solely from the viewpoint of the person to whom it is an important day.

Advertising scripts

Study the script of the advertisement reproduced on pages 136 and 137.

1 Discuss the headline. Why has that particular headline been chosen? Discuss alternatives and compare their effectiveness.

2 Discuss the language that is used in the rest of the advertisement. What impression does the advertising copy-writer want the reader to get of a Royal Marines officer? How does the language that he has chosen help him to convey this impression?

3 What are the various points that are made in the advertisement? Why are they arranged in that particular order?

4 At what sort of person is this advertisement aimed? Do you think it is a successful advertisement? Explain why.

5 Do you think this script would be suitable for a television commercial? How would you adapt it for television? Draw two columns and label one Sound and the other Vision. Write a television commercial based on this script.

6 Study a number of advertisements in one particular magazine. Is there any similarity in the way the advertising copy-writers try to attract the attention of the magazine's readers? Choose an advertisement from the magazine, which you think is particularly effective and explain why.

Sound scripts

We have been considering a variety of different types of script in the course of this unit. We come finally to the sound-script — that written or adapted for radio broadcasting, for recording or simply for reading aloud. In writing a sound-script, the author has to bear in mind all the time the fact that his audience has to come to terms with his story without the benefit of any kind of visual aid. Unlike its stage or screen counterpart, the radio play must convey *everything* by means of words, sound effects and — perhaps — appropriate music. From this point of view, the opening of a sound play is most important: its job is to set the scene, to establish the tone, even to define the characters in such a way that the audience will be in no doubt as to what is going on. Here are the openings of two radio-plays by a man who was master of the art — Giles Cooper. The first is from *The Disagreeable Oyster*:

ANNOUNCER: This is the BBC Third Programme. We present a play by Giles Cooper entitled, 'The Disagreeable Oyster'.

BUNDY: You can say that again.

ANNOUNCER: 'The Disagreeable Oyster'.

BUNDY: They do disagree with me, but how was I to know when I stood on the steps of the Rosedene Family and Commercial Hotel, thinking that the world was my oyster that . . .

BUNDY MINOR: Begin at the beginning.

BUNDY: And the beginning is at twelve o'clock on a Saturday morning in my office at Craddock's Calculators Ltd.. It is not a nice office, even the typing pool have a narrow view of St. Paul's, but poor old Bundy . . .

BUNDY MINOR: My name, Mervyn Bundy . . .

BUNDY: Deputy Head of Costing, has to put up with an office looking out on an air shaft, and all I can see is the upstairs part of a mercantile bank . . .

BUNDY MINOR: Well?

BUNDY: That's the beginning. I'm sitting at my desk on a fine May morning, wondering whether it's worth starting anything else before the week-end begins.

(*Door opens noisily*)

GUNN: Bundy! Good man, Bundy, glad you're still here.

BUNDY: Yes, Mr Gunn?

GUNN: Bundy, there's a crisis, pin your ears back and listen.

BUNDY MINOR: Mr Gunn has ginger hair growing out of *his* ears.

GUNN: C.C.W.'s Stoddeshunt works have just rung through to say that there's an inconsistent error in the V.V.X. machine they bought from us. They're working overtime this week on an export contract with a dirty big penalty clause. Okay, Bundy?

BUNDY: Yes, sir.

GUNN: Right now Maintenance have two men on leave, one sick and one in Pompey.

BUNDY MINOR: Mr Gunn spits a little when he says words like Pompey.

GUNN: That's their full establishment. Okay, Bundy?

BUNDY: Yes, sir.

GUNN: Right, but all the same we've got to get someone up there soonest or we'll lose their account. Okay, Bundy?

BUNDY: Yes, sir.

GUNN: Right, you'll go straight along to Accounts and draw money for expenses, you will then catch the one five, change at Leicester for Stoddeshunt. You will go to the C.C.W. works and ask for Mr. Rigg. He'll show you the machine and you will correct the error. Right?

BUNDY: But, sir, I'm Costs, not Maintenance.

GUNN: Great heavens, man, I know that, but this is an emergency. Can't you rise to an emergency?

BUNDY MINOR: He spits when he says emergency too.

GUNN: The board are worried sick about this C.C.W. account. They'd have recalled the Pompey man, only Pompey's an emergency too. Now don't stand there dabbing yourself with your handkerchief, man. Get cracking.

BUNDY: I'll have to tell my wife.

GUNN: Ring her up.

BUNDY: I might have to stay the night.

GUNN: You will, I know the trains.

BUNDY: I've no things.

GUNN: Buy them, get yourself a toothbrush, pyjamas, bedroom slippers, anything you like when you get there. Here's a chit for the cashier; I'll make it out for thirty pounds. Okay, Bundy?

BUNDY: Yes, sir.

GUNN: Right, and whatever you do, don't miss that train.

(*Door slams*)

BUNDY: I haven't slept away from home for twenty-two years but I couldn't tell him that.

(*Fade in ringing tone of telephone*)

BUNDY MINOR: That's my telephone on the rickety table in my hall. I can hear the sunlight sending a long shaft down from the landing window, I can hear the carpet breathing dust.

(*Ringing tone stops. Receiver lifted*)

ALICE (*distort*): Hullo, who's that? My husband's out.

BUNDY: Alice, it's me, it's Mer.

ALICE: Is something wrong?

BUNDY: No, no, but I've got to go away for the night for the firm. It's an emergency.

ALICE: For the night?

BUNDY: Yes, and I've got to buy a toothbrush and a pair of pyjamas. I'll wear my mackintosh as a dressing-gown.

ALICE: But what about me? I shall be all alone.

BUNDY: I know, darling, but it can't be helped. It's an emergency. I'll be back tomorrow morning, don't forget to put the chain on the door.

ALICE: But who will get the coal, and who will empty the rubbish from the kitchen?

BUNDY: I will, Alice, I will, tomorrow.

ALICE: And bread, I want a wrapped loaf and the shops are shut.

(*Train whistles.*)

BUNDY: I'll get some in Stoddeshunt, but now I must catch the train. Goodbye, Alice, look after yourself, goodbye.

from 'The Disagreeable Oyster' by Giles Cooper

1   In the published version of this play, the author tells us that 'Mervyn Bundy, the principal character, has been divided into two parts, Bundy Major and Bundy Minor. This is partly because he has a lot to say to himself and partly because some of what he says would never be said by the Bundy we see walking about in the streets, this being Bundy

Major, who is nearly always unaware of the existence of Bundy Minor. Minor, on the other hand, is only too well aware of Bundy Major, being inside him and unable to get out'. How effective do you think this sort of device is? Does it have anything in common with that of a narrator linking the different episodes of a story? Could it be employed in any other type of writing (script or otherwise)?

2   What is the effect of the very opening of this extract?

3   How does Giles Cooper help our visual imagination to function as we listen to his play?

4   How is the tone of the piece established?

5   What advantages do radio plays have over stage plays in the matter of the swift and frequent movement from one scene to another? How does Giles Cooper exploit these advantages?

6   How well does Giles Cooper establish the characters of Bundy, Gunn and Alice in this short passage?

Here now is the opening of Cooper's *Mathry Beacon*:

(*A trumpet plays, and out of it comes the sound of the deflector and the wind.*)

EVANS: What a God-forsaken end of the world to send men to . . . that first hill like a ham with a cornfield for bread-crumbs, that was high enough . . .

BLICK: And the part like a green arm-chair . . .

EVANS: It was, too, just like that. Along one arm and up over the back we went.

RITA: I thought that'd be the top at any rate. Wasn't expecting that long hummocky bit.

BETSY: They say it's like a sleeping woman from down below.

OLIM: Well developed.

RITA: That'll do, Gunner Olim.

OLIM: Sorry, Bombardier.

EVANS: Put him on a whizzer.

BETSY: On a fizzer . . .

RITA: On a two-five-two.

GANN (*Off*): Get fell in! (*They groan*) Get fell in.

ALL (*Muttering*): Get fell in, get fell in, get fell in.

GANN (*Approaching*): You ought to be there by now! Party shun, as you were, party shun, stand at hip . . . stand-easy. Now my name's Gann, Lieutenant as you see when I bend my shoulder at you. Thirty-five years' service I've got. Gunner, Bombardier, sergeant, colour-sergeant, sergeant-major and there aren't no tricks that I don't know, but you treat me right, I'll treat you right and we'll all muck in and get on with the job, any questions?

BETSY: What is the job, sir?

GANN: This place here is known as Mathry Beacon. It is two thousand five hundred feet above the sea which is at what is known as sea-level. It is five miles from the road, eight miles from a village and nobody ever comes here except us, which is why volunteers were asked for because you won't be able to get away until relieved. Any questions?

BLICK: What's the job, sir?

GANN: An educated man. What's your name?

BLICK: 703 Gunner Blick A., sir.

GANN: Why aren't you commissioned, an educated man?

BLICK: I wasn't asked, sir.

GANN: Nor me, nor me. Told I was; ordered and I obeyed just as I always do. Any questions?

EVANS: We'd like to know the job please, sir?

GANN: A Welshman, eh? Name?

EVANS: 666 Gunner Evans M., sir.

GANN: The mark of the beast, man, be careful. Interpreter's what you'll be; telling us what the locals say. Once in Kowloon we had an interpreter ate mice. Any questions? (*Pause*) None? Don't you have a question, Sambo?

OLIM: 584 Gunner Olim J., sir.

GANN: Quite right, quite right. I took advantage of this man's colour to address a jocular remark to him and he put me in my place as I deserved. That won't do you any harm, Gunner Olim, nor two-pennorth of good neither. What were you in civilian life?

OLIM: I played a trumpet in a dance-band, sir.

GANN: Got it here?

OLIM: Yes, sir.

GANN: Have a concert one night. Any questions?

RITA: Only what we're going to do, sir.

GANN: Very good, Bombardier. What's your name?

RITA: Bleening.

GANN: Sir.

RITA: Sir.

GANN: And yours?

BETSY: Betsy, please, mister.

(*Laughter*)

GANN: Quiet! Or I'll have you doubling round the barrack square
the moment you've dug one out of the hillside. What's your
other name, Betsy?

BETSY: Ling, please, sir.

GANN (*sings*): 'The bells of Hell go ting-a-ling-a-ling for you and
not for me, for me the angels sing-a-ling-a-ling, they've got the
goods for me.' Very good indeed, now, why you're here,
which none of you seem to take much interest in. Up on the hill
behind us you will see a machine in an emplacement. That
machine is known as the Watling Deflector because it was
invented by an inventor by the name of Watling and because it
is intended to deflect the enemy rockets known as V2s. V
standing for Victory of course, in this case Enemy Victory,
known to us as Defeat. Any questions?

EVANS: How does it work, sir?

GANN: How it works you'll be told in time. When you fall out
from here you will take your kits to your huts according to
whether you're male or female members of the battery. I do not
want to see the one in the other or the other in the one. Why
not, Evans?

EVANS: Well sir, I suppose sir . . .

GANN: He doesn't know, tell him the next man . . . Olim.

OLIM: Because it's not allowed, sir.

GANN: That is a correct answer and the reason it's not allowed is
because. Did you ever see a rhinoceros?

OLIM: Yes, sir.

GANN: And what did it have?

OLIM: Mine didn't have nothing, sir, it was in a zoo.

GANN: Wrong, next man, educated man, what's a rhinoceros got
that you haven't got?

BLICK: A horn on the end of its nose.

(*Laughter*)

    from 'Mathry Beacon' by Giles Cooper

1   In what ways does this opening differ from that of *The Disagreeable Oyster*? Which seems to you the more naturalistic? Which the closer to the opening of a stage play?

2   Are there any points in this extract where Giles Cooper uses a character to act as a kind of narrator?

3   How does he help us visualise not only the setting and background but also the grouping of the characters here?

4   Is any of the characters in this extract established as firmly as Bundy, Gunn or Alice in the opening of *The Disagreeable Oyster*?

5   Make a detailed comparison of these two openings. Which seems to you the more successful? Why?

6   In groups, rehearse and produce a polished tape-recording of one or both of the Giles Cooper extracts.

7   Make your own sound-adaptation of an episode from either a prose narrative (short story or novel) or a stage-script.

7 Speeches and talks

Men and brothers

'Oh, my friends, the down-trodden operatives of Coketown! Oh, my friends and fellow-countrymen, the slaves of an iron-handed and a grinding despotism! Oh, my friends and fellow-sufferers, and fellow-workmen, and fellow-men! I tell you that the hour is come, when we must rally round one another as one united power, and crumble into dust the oppressors that too long have battened upon the plunder of our families, upon the sweat of our brows, upon the labour of our hands, upon the strength of our sinews, upon the God-created glorious rights of humanity, and upon the holy and eternal privileges of brotherhood!'

'Good!' 'Hear, hear, hear!' 'Hurrah!' and other cries, arose in many voices from various parts of the densely-crowded and suffocatingly-close hall, in which the orator, perched on a stage, delivered himself of this and what other froth and fume he had in him. He had declaimed himself into a violent heat, and he was as hoarse as he was hot. By dint of roaring at the top of his voice under a flaring gaslight, clenching his fists, knitting his brows, setting his teeth, and pounding with his arms, he had taken so much out of himself by this time, that he was brought to a stop, and called for a glass of water . . .

The orator having refreshed himself, wiped his corrugated forehead from left to right several times with his handkerchief folded into a pad, and concentrated all his revived forces in a sneer of great disdain and bitterness.

'But, oh, my friends and brothers! Oh, men and Englishmen, the down-trodden operatives of Coketown! What shall we say of that man — that working-man, that I should find it necessary so to libel the glorious name — who, being practically and well acquainted with the grievances and wrongs of you, the injured pith and marrow of this land, and having heard you, with a noble and majestic unanimity that will make tyrants tremble, resolve for to subscribe to the funds of the United Aggregate Tribunal, and to abide by the injunctions issued by that body for your benefit, whatever they may be – what, I ask you, will you say of that working-man, since such I must acknowledge him to be, who, at such a time, deserts his post, and sells his flag; who, at such a time, turns a traitor and a craven and a recreant; who, at such a time, is not ashamed to make you the dastardly and humiliating avowal that he will hold himself aloof, and will *not* be one of those associated in the gallant stand for freedom and for right?'

The assembly was divided at this point. There were some groans and hisses, but the general sense of honour was much too strong for the condemnation of a man unheard. 'Be sure you're right, Slackbridge!' 'Put him up!' 'Let's hear him!' Such things were said on many sides. Finally, one strong voice called out, 'Is the man heer? If the man's heer, Slackbridge, let's hear the man himself, 'stead o' yo.' Which was received with a round of applause.

Slackbridge, the orator, looked about him with a withering smile, and, holding out his right hand at arm's length (as the manner of all Slackbridges is) to still the thundering sea, waited until there was a profound silence.

'Oh, my friends and fellow-men!' said Slackbridge then, shaking his head with violent scorn, 'I do not wonder that you, the prostrate sons of labour, are incredulous of the existence of such a man. But he who sold his birthright for a mess of pottage existed, and Judas Iscariot existed, and Castlereagh existed, and this man exists!'

from 'Hard Times' by Charles Dickens

The extract from *Hard Times*, which you have just read, shows an experienced orator manipulating his audience. Consider the extent to which the speaker achieves his ends through gesture and manner as well as by his use of language.

Preparing a speech

Speeches need careful preparation. Very few orators – even the most experienced ones – deliver a speech 'off the cuff', though their delivery may be so skilled that they may be able to create the impression that the speech conveys their immediate thoughts, rather than a careful, pre-selected arrangement of them. The thorough preparation of a speech can involve not only assembling your thoughts in the order in which you want to present them, but deciding exactly how you are going to present them – at which points in your speech you are going to pause or which words and phrases you are going to stress, in order to draw your audience's attention to a particular point or to influence them in a particular way.

The extent of the preparation will vary according to the type of speech, the audience for whom it is intended and the occasion on which it is to be delivered. Sometimes it will be sufficient for the speaker merely to write down a series of headings to remind him of the main points and the order in which he is going to present them. At other times he will write out his speech in full, making notes on where he is going to pause and how he is going to stress certain points.

The structure of the speech and the language used will depend upon the speaker's purpose. The speaker whose intention is simply to convey information or to put forward an argument that he wishes his audience to consider and either accept or reject as they think fit, will construct his speech differently from the speaker whose purpose is to convince his audience of the rightness of his argument or to appeal to their emotions in order to get them to act in a particular way. Similarly, if the speaker's aim is to entertain rather than to inform, then the structure and language of his speech will be chosen accordingly. As you study the speeches in this unit consider the various ways in which they are constructed and how the authors have manipulated language in order to achieve their ends.

Speeches as exhortation and argument

One of the functions of speeches is to *persuade* the audiences to whom they are addressed – to sway them or at least to encourage them perhaps to vote or act in a particular way. Such speeches need to present their arguments clearly and concisely, otherwise there is a danger that the hearers will become lost or bored or alienated. At the same time, it is important that they put across their messages in such a way that there is

no danger of their being misunderstood — and this sometimes means
that repetition and special emphasis are required. The following speech
comes from Shakespeare's play *Richard III*; it is spoken by Henry, Earl of
Richmond, who has returned from exile in France to challenge the
tyrannical king Richard's right to the throne of England. Shakespeare
based it on the actual words Richmond spoke to his troops before the
Battle of Bosworth as they are recorded in contemporary chronicles.

More than I have said, loving countrymen,
The leisure and enforcement of the time
Forbids to dwell upon. Yet remember this:
God and our good cause fight upon our side;
The prayers of holy saints and wronged souls,   5
Like high-reared bulwarks, stand before our faces.
Richard except, those whom we fight against
Had rather have us win than him they follow.
For what is he they follow? Truly, gentlemen,
A bloody tyrant and a homicide;   10
One raised in blood, and one in blood established;
One that made means to come by what he hath,
And slaughtered those that were the means to help him;
A base foul stone, made precious by the foil
Of England's chair, where he is falsely set;   15
One that hath ever been God's enemy.
Then if you fight against God's enemy,
God will in justice ward you as his soldiers;
If you do sweat to put a tyrant down,
You sleep in peace, the tyrant being slain;   20
If you do fight against your country's foes,
Your country's fat shall pay your pains the hire;
If you do fight in safeguard of your wives,
Your wives shall welcome home the conquerors;
If you do free your children from the sword   25
Your children's children quits it in your age.
Then, in the name of God and all these rights,
Advance your standards, draw your willing swords.
For me, the ransom of my bold attempt
Shall be this cold corpse on the earth's cold face;   30
But if I thrive, the gain of my attempt

The least of you shall share his part thereof.
Sound drums and trumpets boldly and cheerfully –
God and Saint George! Richmond and Victory!
  from 'Richard III' by William Shakespeare

1 The speech begins rather oddly, as if Richmond has already been speaking to his men at some length. 'I haven't the time or the opportunity now to say more,' he declares, 'but I want you to remember this at least. . . .' – and so he proceeds with what he wants to impress on them. Read through the speech carefully several times and then try in your own words, and in not more than two or three sentences, to summarise the main points of Richmond's argument.

2 Look carefully at lines 9 – 16 where Richmond dwells on the character of his enemy. What is the effect of the following features of this passage:
(a) the opening question 'For what is he they follow?'
(b) the repeated word-formula 'One . . . One that . . . One that . . .' (lines 11, 12, 16)? How do you imagine such lines ought to be spoken?

3 Now look at lines 17 – 26 where he suggests what benefits will ensue to them if his men will only confront such an enemy. Where can you find in these lines further examples of repeated word-formulae? What is their effect? How should they be spoken?

4 How in lines 16 and 17 does Richmond create a link or bridge between these two passages, and – in so doing – reinforce the logical structure of his argument?

5 Which word in line 27 indicates that he is coming to the climax of his argument?

6 What is the effect of the last two lines of this speech? Do they add anything to the argument or do they serve some other purpose?

7 What sort of response do you imagine Richmond would have received from his troops at different points in this speech?

8 What, in sum, would you say is the speaker's intention in this passage?

The notation and preparation of speeches

In your analysis of Richmond's speech from *Richard III*, you will have already touched – albeit in a limited way – on two crucial aspects of speechmaking: the speaker's awareness of his audience and its reaction to his words and his careful preparation not only of what he is going to say but also of how he is going to say it. These two facets of speechmaking are closely related – correct assessment of the mood of his hearers will determine just how and in what tone a speaker will approach them. An experienced speaker will plan in advance not only where the chief climaxes of his speech are to occur but also how most effectively to communicate them, by means of dramatic pauses or gestures; of variations in the pace of his delivery, in the pitch of his voice or in the loudness with which he speaks; of steady crescendo or diminuendo in volume; of the special emphasis of certain words and phrases; of sudden outbursts or moments of quietness; of variations in tone, from a gentle crooning to a staccato bark. Sir Winston Churchill, for instance, was in the habit of mapping out the delivery of his important wartime speeches in advance so that he could be sure of making exactly the right impact with his words.

Imagine now that you are Richmond about to deliver the speech you have been examining earlier in this unit. Write it out in full, indicating how you propose to speak it. You may either devise your own code or symbols for different aspects of your delivery or you could perhaps employ the sort of symbols used in musical notation. For instance:

accel	=	get faster	◁	=	get louder
rit	=	get slower	▷	=	get softer
p	=	soft	⌒	=	pause
f	=	loud	>	=	stress
sfz	=	suddenly loud			

Broadcast speeches

The following two speeches were both radio broadcasts, delivered during the Second World War. Churchill's speech, known as 'The Fourth Climacteric', was broadcast on June 22, 1941, and Forster's radio talk was one of three anti-Nazi broadcasts, delivered during 1940. The intention behind the speeches is the same – to support the British war-effort against the Nazis – but their tone and content contrast strongly. As you read through them – and it would be a good idea to try reading aloud in a manner and voice that you consider appropriate – think of what effect these speakers were aiming to make on their listeners.

A world broadcast on the German invasion of Russia, June 22, 1941

1   I have taken occasion to speak to you tonight because we have reached one of the climacterics of the war. The first of these intense turning-points was a year ago when France fell prostrate under the German hammer, and when we had to face the storm alone. The second was when the Royal Air Force beat the Hun raiders out of the daylight air, and thus warded off the Nazi invasion of our island while we were still ill-armed and ill-prepared. The third turning-point was when the President and Congress of the United States passed the Lease-and-Lend enactment, devoting nearly 2 000 millions sterling of the wealth of the New World to help us to defend our liberties and their own. Those were the three climacterics. The fourth is now upon us.

2   At four o'clock this morning Hitler attacked and invaded Russia. All his usual formalities of perfidy were observed with scrupulous technique. A non-aggression treaty had been solemnly signed and was in force between the two countries. No complaint had been made by Germany of its non-fulfilment. Under its cloak of false confidence, the German armies drew up in immense strength along a line which stretches from the White Sea to the Black Sea; and their air fleets and armoured divisions slowly and methodically took their stations. Then, suddenly, without declaration of war, without even an ultimatum, German bombs rained down from the air upon the Russian cities, the German troops violated the frontiers; and an hour later the German Ambassador, who till the night before was lavishing his assurances of friendship, almost of alliance, upon the Russian, called upon the Russian Foreign Minister to tell him that a state of war existed between Germany and Russia.

Thus was repeated on a far larger scale the same kind of outrage against every form of signed compact and international faith which we have witnessed in Norway, Denmark, Holland and Belgium, and which Hitler's accomplice and jackal Mussolini so faithfully imitated in the case of Greece.

All this was no surprise to me. In fact I gave clear and precise warnings to Stalin of what was coming. I gave him warning as I have given warning to others before. I can only hope that this warning did not fall unheeded. All we know at present is that the Russian people are defending their native soil and that their leaders have called upon them to resist to the utmost.

Hitler is a monster of wickedness, insatiable in his lust for blood and plunder. Not content with having all Europe under his heel, or else terrorized into various forms of abject submission, he must now carry his work of butchery and desolation among the vast multitudes of Russia and of Asia. The terrible military machine, which we and the rest of the civilized world so foolishly, so supinely, so insensately allowed the Nazi gangsters to build up year by year from almost nothing, cannot stand idle lest it rust or fall to pieces. It must be in continual motion, grinding up human lives and trampling down the homes and the rights of hundreds of millions of men. Moreover it must be fed, not only with flesh but with oil.

So now this bloodthirsty guttersnipe must launch his mechanised armies upon new fields of slaughter, pillage and devastation. Poor as are the Russian peasants, work-men and soldiers, he must steal from them their daily bread; he must devour their harvests; he must rob them of the oil which drives their ploughs; and thus produce a famine without example in human history. And even the carnage and ruin which his victory, should he gain it — he has not gained it yet — will bring upon the Russian people, will itself be only a stepping-stone to the attempt to plunge the 400 000 000 or 500 000 000 who live in China, and the 350 000 000 who live in India, into that bottomless pit of human degradation over which the diabolic emblem of the Swastika flaunts itself. It is not too much to say here this summer evening that the lives and happiness of 1 000 000 000 additional people are now menaced with brutal Nazi violence. That is enough to make us hold our breath. But presently I shall show you something else that lies behind, and something that touches very nearly the life of Britain and of the United States.

3 The Nazi regime is indistinguishable from the worst features of Communism. It is devoid of all theme and principle except appetite and racial domination. It excels all forms of human wickedness in the efficiency of its cruelty and ferocious aggression. No one has been a more consistent opponent of Communism than

I have for the last twenty-five years. I will unsay no word that I have spoken about it. But all this fades away before the spectacle which is now unfolding. The past with its crimes, its follies and its tragedies, flashes away. I see the Russian soldiers standing on the threshold of their native land, guarding the fields which their fathers have tilled from time immemorial. I see them guarding their homes where mothers and wives pray – ah yes, for there are times when all pray – for the safety of their loved ones, the return of the bread-winner, of their champion, of their protector. I see the 10 000 villages of Russia, where the means of existence was wrung so hardly from the soil, but where there are still primordial human joys, where maidens laugh and children play. I see advancing upon all this in hideous onslaught the Nazi war machine, with its clanking, heel-clicking, dandified Prussian officers, its crafty expert agents fresh from the cowing and tying-down of a dozen countries. I see also the dull, drilled, docile, brutish masses of the Hun soldiery plodding on like a swarm of crawling locusts. I see the German bombers and fighters in the sky, still smarting from many a British whipping, delighted to find what they believe is an easier and a safer prey.

Behind all this glare, behind all this storm, I see that small group of villainous men who plan, organise and launch this cataract of horrors upon mankind. And then my mind goes back across the years to the days when the Russian armies were our allies against the same deadly foe; when they fought with so much valour and constancy, and helped to gain a victory from all share in which, alas, they were – through no fault of ours – utterly cut off. I have lived through all this, and you will pardon me if I express my feelings and the stir of old memories.

But now I have to declare the decision of His Majesty's Government – and I feel sure it is a decision in which the great Dominions will, in due course, concur – for we must speak out now at once, without a day's delay. I have to make the declaration, but can you doubt what our policy will be? We have but one aim and one single, irrevocable purpose. We are resolved to destroy Hitler and every vestige of the Nazi regime. From this nothing will turn us – nothing. We will never parley, we will never negotiate with Hitler or any of his gang. We shall fight him by land, we shall fight him by sea, we shall fight him in the air, until with God's help we have rid the earth of his shadow and liberated its peoples from his yoke. Any man or state who fights on against Nazidom will have our aid. Any man or state who marches with Hitler is our foe. This applies not only to organised States but to all representatives of that vile race of quislings who make themselves the tools and agents of the Nazi regime against their fellow-countrymen and the lands of their birth. They — these quislings — like the Nazi leaders themselves, if not disposed of by their fellow-countrymen, which would save trouble, will be delivered by us on the morrow of victory to the justice of the Allied tribunals. That is our policy and that is our declaration. It follows, therefore, that we shall give whatever help we can to Russia and the Russian people. We shall appeal to all our friends and allies in every part of the world to take the same course and pursue it, as we shall, faithfully and steadfastly to the end.

We have offered the Government of Soviet Russia any technical or economic assistance which is in our power, and which is likely to be of service to them. We shall bomb Germany by day as well as by night in ever-increasing measure, casting upon them month by month a heavier discharge of bombs, and making the German people taste and gulp each month a sharper dose of the miseries they have showered upon mankind. It is noteworthy that only yesterday the Royal Air Force, fighting inland over French territory, cut down with very small loss to themselves twenty-eight of the Hun fighting machines in the air above the French soil they have invaded, defiled and profess to hold. But this is only a beginning. From now forward the main expansion of our Air Force proceeds with gathering speed. In another six months the weight of the help we are receiving from the United States in war materials of all kinds, and especially in heavy bombers, will begin to tell.

This is no class war, but a war in which the whole British Empire and Commonwealth of Nations is engaged without distinction of race, creed or party. It is not for me to speak of the action of the United States, but this I will say: if Hitler imagines that his attack on Soviet Russia will cause the slightest division of aims or slackening of effort in the great democracies who are resolved upon his doom, he is woefully mistaken. On the contrary, we shall be fortified and encouraged in our efforts to rescue mankind from his tyranny. We shall be strengthened and not weakened in determination and in resources.

4   This is no time to moralise on the follies of countries and Governments which have allowed themselves to be struck down one by one, when by united action they could have saved themselves and saved the world from this catastrophe. But when I spoke a few minutes ago of Hitler's blood-lust and the hateful appetites which have impelled or lured him on his Russian adventure, I said there was one deeper motive behind his outrage. He wishes to destroy the Russian power because he hopes that if he succeeds in this, he will be able to bring back the main strength of his Army and Air Force from the east and hurl it upon this island, which he knows he must conquer or suffer the penalty of his crimes. His invasion of Russia is no more than prelude to an attempted invasion of the British Isles. He hopes, no doubt, that all this may be accomplished before the winter comes, and that he can overwhelm Great Britain before the Fleet and air-power of the United States may intervene. He hopes that he may once again repeat, upon a greater scale than ever before, that process of destroying his enemies one by one, by which he has so long thrived and prospered, and that then the scene will be clear for the final act, without which all his conquests will be in vain — namely, the subjugation of the Western hemisphere to his will and to his system.

The Russian danger is therefore our danger, and the danger of the United States, just as the cause of any Russian fighting for his hearth and home is the cause of free men and free peoples in every quarter of the globe. Let us learn the lessons already taught by such cruel experience. Let us redouble our exertions, and strike with united strength while life and power remain.

from 'The War Speeches' by Sir Winston Churchill

What would Germany do to us?

What would the Nazis do to civilization in these islands and in the Empire if they won?

I don't suggest that conditions here are perfect . . . but . . . they are paradise compared with the conditions in Germany, and heaven compared with the conditions which Germany would impose on us if she beat us. I want to describe what she would do to us if she got the chance.

You may say: 'Oh, but how do you know? No doubt the Nazis would impose appalling peace terms on us if they won, but why should they interfere with our culture?' My answer to that is: 'I do know, because I have the record of what they have done to other countries, particularly to Czechoslovakia and to Poland.' Destruction of national culture is part of their programme of conquest. In Czechoslovakia, for instance, they have barred the operas of Smetana and the plays of Capek. They have revised school books, falsified Czech history, forbidden the singing of Czech national songs, and subsidized German educational institutions, for which the Czechs have to pay. In Poland, the fate of culture has been still more tragic, since Poland is a conquered country: their conduct in Poland is the model which the Nazis would follow if they got over here. Listen, for instance, how they have treated the University of Cracow – and then put for 'Cracow' 'Oxford' or any other university which you know. Last November, one hundred and seventy professors and teachers at Cracow were summoned by the chief of the Gestapo to the hall of the university and placed under arrest on the grounds that they were continuing their work without Nazi permission. They were sent straight off to concentration camps in Germany, where sixteen of them died, and their places were filled by Nazi nominees. I know Cracow. I have had friends in the university there of whom I can get no news. They have welcomed me to their charming little flats overlooking the green boulevards: they have shown me their noble city with its great Catholic churches and its marvellous fortress. Owing to their kindness and hospitality, it has happened that Cracow has become for me a symbol of Nazi bullying on the Continent, and I can hardly see its name without trembling with rage. I mention it now – that lost and lovely place – because one needs to visualize in these terrible times. It does not convey much if I say 'The Nazis would reorganise and re-staff our educational system.' It does convey something if I say 'They would treat Oxford as they have treated Cracow.' They are stamping out culture everywhere in Poland, so far as they can. They consider it their mission to do so, on the ground that the Poles are naturally inferior to Germans. 'A Pole is a Pole,' writes a Nazi journalist, 'and any attempt at familiarity must be rebuffed.'

Let us now consider the effect of a Nazi victory upon our civilization.

Our press, our publishing and printing trades, our universities and the rest of our educational system would be instantly controlled. So would theatres, cinemas, and the wireless. The British Government (assuming that one remained) would be held responsible for their conduct, and have to punish them if they did anything which annoyed Berlin. There would be complete remodelling. In these respects, the methods adopted in Czechoslovakia and Poland would be followed, and with the maximum of brutality; the joy of baiting Englishmen in England would be intoxicating. Germanization would probably not be attempted. But the Gestapo and the rest of the occupying force would, of course, import such Nazi culture as was necessary for their spiritual sustenance, and we should have to pay for German libraries and German schools, into which, as members of an inferior race, we should not be allowed to go.

What about our literature? The fate of individual writers would be hard. Those of any eminence would probably be interned and shot. This, however painful to themselves, would not, it is true, be a great blow to literature, for by the time writers have become eminent they have usually done their best work. What would matter, what would be disastrous, is the intimidation of our younger writers – men and women in their twenties and thirties, who have not yet had the chance to express themselves. The invaders would take good care to frighten or cajole them. Forbidden to criticize their conquerors, forbidden to recall the past glories of their country, or to indulge that free movement of the mind which is necessary to the creative art, they would be confined to trivialities, or to spreading their masters' opinions.

Would they try to burn English books too? I don't think so. It would mean too big a blaze. We should probably be left with our existing libraries and allowed to read our classics in such spare time as we possessed. I do think though that a different interpretation of English literature would be attempted in our schools. They would put it to our young people that our best writers were Nazis at heart, and so try to warp their minds . . . .

Those seem to me the chief cultural points in a Nazi conquest — and you will remember that I am keeping to this particular aspect, and not talking about politics and economics. They want our land, it is true; they want our money — sure. But they also want to alter our civilization until it is in line with their own. If my view of them is right, they cannot *help* doing this: it is, so to speak, their fate. They have identified civilization with the State, and the National Socialist State cannot be secure until no civilization exists except the particular one which it approves.

This being so, I think we have got to go on with this hideous fight. I cannot see how we are to make terms with Hitler, much as I long for peace. For one thing, he never keeps his word; for another, he tolerates no way of looking at life except his own way. A peace which was the result of a Nazi victory would surely not differ from a Nazi war. Germans would no longer be killed, but they would go on killing others until no one survived to criticize them. In the end, they might achieve world-domination and institute a culture. But what sort of culture would it be? What would they have to work with? For you cannot go on destroying lives and living processes without destroying your own life. If you continue to be greedy and dense, if you make power and not understanding your aim, if, as a French friend of mine puts it, you erect 'a pyramid of appetites on a foundation of stupidity', you kill the impulse to create. Creation is disinterested. Creation means passionate understanding. Creation lies at the heart of civilization like fire in the heart of the earth. Around it are gathered its cooler allies, criticism, the calm use of the intellect, informing the mass and moulding it into shape. The intellect is not everything — the Nazis are quite right there. But no one can insult the intellect as they do without becoming sterile and cruel. We know their cruelty. We should see their sterility if this orgy of destruction were to stop, and they turned at their Fuehrer's command to the production of masterpieces.

In this difficult day when so many of us are afraid: in this day when so many brave plans have gone wrong and so many devices have jammed, it is a comfort to remember that violence has so far never worked. Even when it seems to conquer, it fails in the long run. This failure may be due to the Divine Will. It can also be ascribed to the strange nature of Man, who refuses to live by bread alone, and is the only animal who has attempted to understand his surroundings.

   from 'Three Anti-Nazi Broadcasts' by E. M. Forster

   1   Consider the structure of thought in each of these broadcasts. Churchill's speech is here divided into four numbered sections. Provide a title for each of these sections and state clearly what you take to be the main issue for which Churchill wishes to gain support. The content of Forster's broadcast can similarly be summarised in four short statements. What issue is he primarily concerned with?
   2   Discuss Churchill's speech as the utterances of a national leader. What impact does he wish to make on his listeners? Does he aim to affect them emotionally as well as to convey a political statement? Do you find that he ever sacrifices clarity of thought for emotional impact?
   3   Both these broadcasts include personal reminiscence, Forster's much more than Churchill's. Do they use a personal tone for the same purpose? Why is there so much more personal reminiscence in Forster's broadcast?
   4   Compare Churchill's description of the Russian people with Forster's description of Cracow. For what purpose is each of these descriptions developed?
   5   Which of these two speakers presents himself as essentially 'a reasonable man'? Which most clearly assumes that his listeners will be in total agreement with him? Find sentences in the speeches which support your views.
   6   'We shall never parley, we will never negotiate with Hitler or any of his gang. We shall fight him by land, we shall fight him by sea, we shall fight him in the air, until with God's help we have rid the earth of his shadow and liberated its peoples from his yoke.'
'This being so, I think we have got to go on with this hideous fight. I cannot see how we are to make terms with Hitler, much as I long for peace. For one thing, he never keeps his word; for another, he tolerates no way of looking at life except his own way.' Compare and contrast the sentence structure, the thought and the tone of these two extracts from the speeches. What does your comparison show you about the manner in which Churchill and Forster make their points?
   7   How does Churchill refer to the enemy? Contrast his method of referring to them with the manner in which Forster talks about the Germans.
Finally, choose a topic which would be likely to arouse some feelings, for example, the position of women in society or the presence of

immigrants in the country, and prepare and deliver to the rest of the class two very short speeches. One of these should be chatty and thoughtful, appealing to reason and humane feelings, and the other should be designed to stir the emotions of your audience and urge them to take action. Distinguish the various techniques that different members of the class use.

Presenting a point of view

In this extract from the speech which he gave when opening an extension building of the Manchester College of Science and Technology, H. R. H. Prince Philip puts forward a particular point of view.

We live in a most remarkable country. Throughout Great Britain's history, national prosperity has always resulted from particular skill and ability in industry and commerce backed by inquiring minds. Yet only occasionally has it been thought necessary to make any effort to help with the education and training of those men on whom industrial and commercial prosperity so obviously depends.

This strange reluctance to admit the importance of science and technology is nothing new. As long ago as the early seventeenth century Sir Francis Bacon wrote: 'It is esteemed a kind of dishonour to learning to descend into an inquiry upon matters mechanical.' While in the nineteenth century a certain churchman wrote: 'The advantages of a classical education are twofold: it enables us to look with contempt upon those who have not shared its advantages, and it fits us for places of emolument, both in this world and the next.' He obviously had much the same outlook as the journalist of the twentieth century who wrote a short time ago that: 'Scientists are no doubt necessary, but it would surely be desirable that they should be kept under control by people who have what until now have been regarded as civilised values.' The implication seems to be that anyone who is sufficiently misguided to become a scientist is automatically an irresponsible citizen without 'civilised values'.

But the fact remains that without properly trained and educated scientists and technologists, industry and agriculture, medicine and nuclear power, defence and rockets would very soon shrivel and disappear. We could probably do quite well without some of these things, but our days as a modern civilised state with a reasonably high standard of living would be numbered. The health of this country, the prosperity of this country and the defence of this country depend for their development upon the ideas of scientists and upon the skill of technologists to convert those ideas into practical and useful hardware. This is one of the hard facts of modern life and the more we can do to ensure that this country has enough properly trained and educated scientists and technologists the sooner we shall get ourselves out of this present state of lagging production, which is a polite way of saying chronic poverty.

It is perfectly true that the great pioneers of British industry were largely self-taught men. You will also find that the majority of the men who control industry in this country today did not have the benefit of a University education. But we cannot go on leaving it to chance to produce the men we need for research, development and administration if we wish to improve, let alone retain, our standard of living. This is not a matter of keeping up with the Joneses, it is a matter of remaining solvent. We are, certainly, going through a difficult period just now, but I firmly believe that the stock of talent, skill and ability which has flowered so often before in the history of these islands is as great as ever. I also believe that any man who, for any reason, is not making the best use of his share of that stock is wasting his own time and his country's most precious raw material.

from 'Prince Philip Speaks' (ed. Richard Ollard)

The following exercises are designed to help you to understand first the content, then the structure of the speech. Work in pairs.

1   Discuss the point of view that Prince Philip is expressing. If you had to choose a title for this extract what would it be?

2   You are students at the college. One of you heard this part of the speech, the other missed it. Take it in turns to be the one who heard it and explain to your friend what Prince Philip said.

3   You are two journalists. One of you has been asked by your editor to write as sensational a report as possible on what Prince Philip said, the other has been asked by his editor to write a straightforward report to

inform the readership of the content of Prince Philip's speech. Write your two reports and write headlines for them, then compare them.

4   Examine the structure of this part of Prince Philip's speech. Consider the four paragraphs in turn. Decide what particular point is being made in each one and summarise it in a single sentence. Compare your summaries with those of other pairs, decide whose summaries are the most accurate and then discuss how one point leads to another and enables Prince Philip to develop his argument.

5   Choose a topic on which you hold a particular point of view — it can be anything from the way British people treat their pets, to the need for our laws to be changed in some way or what is wrong with British football. Produce a list of topic/paragraph headings similar to those you produced when discussing the structure of Prince Philip's speech. Write your speech, then present it to your partner. Discuss it with him and revise it in the light of his comments, before presenting it to the whole group.

This speech is taken from Milton's epic poem *Paradise Lost*. In Book II Satan and the other angels, who have been cast out of heaven, are debating whether or not to hazard another battle for the recovery of heaven. In this speech Beelzebub counsels another course of action.

Thrones and Imperial Powers, off-spring of Heav'n,
Ethereal Vertues; or these Titles now
Must we renounce, and changing stile be call'd
Princes of Hell? For so the popular vote
Inclines, here to continue, and build up here
A growing Empire; doubtless; while we dream,
And know not that the King of Heav'n hath doom'd
This place our dungeon, not our safe retreat
Beyond his Potent arm, to live exempt
From Heav'ns high jurisdiction, in new League
Banded against his Throne, but to remaine
In strictest bondage, though thus farr remov'd,
Under th'inevitable curb, reserv'd
His captive multitude: For he, be sure,
In highth or depth, still first and last will Reign
Sole King, and of his Kingdom lose no part
By our revolt, but over Hell extend
His Empire, and with Iron Scepter rule
Us here, as with his Gold'n those in Heav'n.

What sit we then projecting Peace and Warr?
Warr hath determin'd us, and foil'd with loss
Irreparable; terms of peace yet none
Voutsaf't or sought; for what peace will be giv'n
To us enslav'd, but custody severe,
And stripes, and arbitrary punishment
Inflicted? and what peace can wee return,
But to our power hostility and hate,
Untam'd reluctance, and revenge though slow,
Yet ever plotting how the Conquerour least
May reap his conquest, and may least rejoyce
In doing what we most in suffering feel?
Nor will occasion want, nor shall we need
With dangerous expedition to invade
Heav'n, whose high walls fear no assault or Seige,
Or ambush from the Deep. What if we find
Some easier enterprise? There is a place
(If ancient and prophetic fame in Heav'n
Err not) another World, the happy seat
Of some new Race call'd Man, about this time
To be created like to us, though less
In power and excellence, but favour'd more
Of him who rules above; so was his will
Pronounc't among the Gods, and by an Oath,
That shook Heav'ns whole circumference, confirm'd.
Thither let us bend all our thoughts, to learn
What creatures there inhabit, of what mould,
Or substance, how endu'd, and what thir Power,
And where thir weakness, how attempted best,
By force or suttlety: Though Heav'n be shut,
And Heav'ns high Arbitrator sit secure
In his own strength, this place may lye expos'd
The utmost border of his Kingdom, left
To their defence who hold it: here perhaps
Som advantagious act may be achiev'd
By sudden onset, either with Hell fire
To waste his whole Creation, or possess
All as our own, and drive as wee were driven,
The punie habitants, or if not drive,

Seduce them to our Party, that thir God
May prove thir foe, and with repenting hand
Abolish his own works. This would surpass
Common revenge, and interrupt his Joy
In our Confusion, and our Joy upraise
In his Disturbance; when his darling Sons
Hurl'd headlong to partake with us, shall curse
Thir frail Originals, and faded bliss,
Faded so soon. Advise if this be worth
Attempting, or to sit in darkness here
Hatching vain Empires.

from 'Paradise Lost' Book II by John Milton

1   What is the mood of the audience when Beelzebub rises to address them? What course of action are they favouring?

2   What argument does Beelzebub develop to pour scorn on this suggestion? Which of the words and phrases that he uses are selected to influence his listeners by their emotional effect rather than their appeal to the audience's reason?

3   What alternative course of action does Beelzebub propose? How does he present his argument in favour of it so as to make it appeal to the assembly?

4   One device that Beelzebub uses throughout this speech is the rhetorical question — a question that is asked which the speaker answers himself and which the audience is not expected to answer. Go through the speech and pick out the rhetorical questions. Which of them do you consider to be the most effective? Why?

5   In this speech Milton shows Beelzebub to be a skilled debater. He assesses the mood of the audience accurately and begins, therefore, by stating the reasons for them to reject the course of action that they are at that moment favouring, before going on to state his own case. Choose one of the topics listed below and then write a speech of your own designed to influence an audience that is inclining towards the opposite view to yours. Develop your speech in the way Beelzebub does, first showing the flaws in their viewpoint, before going on to explain your own.

a) Young people of sixteen should be given the vote.
b) Murderers of policemen should be hanged.
c) Compulsory retirement at fifty should be introduced.
d) The school leaving age should be reduced to fourteen.

e) Caning in school should be abolished.
f) Britain should leave the Common Market.
g) The monarchy should be abolished.
h) Violence on television causes violent behaviour.
i) Supplementary benefit should not be paid to strikers or their families.
j) Hospital patients should have to pay for the cost of their board and lodging.

Speeches and talks for entertainment and information

There is often a pronounced difference in mood and tone between speeches delivered 'live' before a group which may or may not be sympathetic towards the speaker and his ideas and those recorded or broadcast without the benefit of audience reaction. The latter, having no apparent need to woo the hostile or rouse up the faithful, are more inclined to adopt a neutral tone, avoiding the rhetorical extremes sometimes required in coping with visible and often vocal audiences. That does not, however, make them any the less speeches or diminish their need to attract and keep the attention of the listeners and to inform and persuade them of a point of view with which they may not immediately sympathise. The following is the text of a special kind of speech – the broadcast talk. True, it does not set out to impress a doctrine on the audience; rather, it is concerned to educate and inform him. Read it carefully and then use the questions which follow to help you analyse its method of working:

Look what you've done you silly gentlemen!

Theories of the development of languages seem to agree that its employment for purposes of factual description and rational argument is the last and highest stage of its evolution. Before that stage was reached it was used to incite action by other people and evoke feelings in them, as in 'clear off' and 'rotten swine'. The earliest form of articulate speech was purely expressive, an uncalculating business of venting the emotions of the speaker, not directed at anyone in particular, or, perhaps, at all, a system of ritualised cries.

Cursing and swearing are the most conspicuous conversational residues of this earliest period in man's history as a discursive being. Now the ordinary repertoire of swearwords is almost exclusively composed of terms connected with religion and sex. 'Damn' and 'hell' are eschatological imperatives, one mentioning the ticket, the other the destination, of a trip to the place of eternal punishment. 'Bloody' we have all been brought up to believe, is a contraction of 'by Our Lady'. I am sorry to say that that piece of homespun etymology is not endorsed by the *Shorter Oxford English Dictionary*. That authoritative work divides the imprecatory use of the word into, first, 'in low English, an epithet expressing detestation' and, secondly, 'an intensive (adverb); very . . . . and no mistake, abominably, desperately, colloquial to c1750, now low English'. Both adjective and adverb are said probably to derive from ''sblood', that is to say, 'Christ's blood', so at least the religious connection is maintained.

Stronger maledictions are of sexual origin and character. Normal and abnormal varieties of sexual intercourse provide the two good old stand-bys. With the preposition 'off' attached they serve as forceful commands to go away. A thing mentioned as the grammatical object of one of these verbs is thereby said to be ruined, spoiled or even destroyed. The sexual parts of the body are the other main source of swearwords. A person who is described as being either a male or a female genital organ is thereby said to be a fool, idiot or generally incompetent person. Where the aim is to convey moral, rather than intellectual, disapproval the person is described as a quantity of excrement. Breasts do not figure much in swearing under that name, but as tits and boobs are used for the makers of silly mistakes and for the silly mistakes that they make. The word boob acquires such a use very naturally from its likeness to booby; a boob is the sort of folly a booby is qualified to perpetrate. I do not really suppose that boob so applied has anything more in common than identity of sound and spelling with its use (usually plural, as a dictionary would say) to refer to the breasts. In the latter sense it must be an up-to-date version of bub or bubby, which comes from the German colloquial bubbi for teat.

Blasphemous swearing is clearly of great antiquity. The first medieval knight to have been dismounted in a joust must have cried 'Zounds' as he hit the greensward. It is not clear to me when low, colloquial, non-medical words of a sexual nature began to be used for purposes of imprecation. There are fine old, improper

168

Anglo-Saxon terms in Chaucer but they seem to have been employed only in a straightforward descriptive way. The miller did not say 'well I'll be swived (or swiven)' when he found out how he had been bamboozled.

The prime purpose of swearing is to express strong unfavourable emotion. It is natural, therefore, that swearwords should be drawn from dangerous, forbidden, consecrated domains. It may be that the supplanting of religion by sex as the supplier of strong language reflects the decline of literal religious belief. Does current sexual permissiveness spell the end of standard obscenity? If so, what will take its place?

It is sometimes said that the two great unmentionables in the present age are death and class. In time to come will the infuriated drivers of non-polluting electrical cars shout 'corpse' and 'putrefy off' at each other at the traffic lights, or foremen (elected, of course, by the factory council) address fumbling neophytes with 'look what you've done, you silly gentlemen'?

Anthony Quinton

1   What is the speaker, Anthony Quinton's purpose in this talk?
2   By what means, in the first paragraph, does he attract the attention of the listener?
3   How does the second paragraph develop the ideas put before us in the first? What is the purpose of the examples Quinton gives?
4   How does the material of the third paragraph grow from what has gone before?
5   How does the speaker keep the interest of his audience in this part of his talk? Is his purpose here entirely serious?
6   What is the central idea of the fifth paragraph? How do the ideas contained in the sixth develop from it?
7   Do you find anything comic or absurd in Quinton's final predictions? In what tone do you suppose he originally delivered this last part of his talk?
8   In general, does the abundance of examples add to or detract from the effectiveness of this piece? Why?
9   The language used here is sometimes difficult to understand. What is the speaker's purpose in employing such language in a basically light-hearted address? Find some examples from the text of complex expressions and decide — once you are sure you understand what they mean — how they add to the overall effect.

Zenocrates & Phryne

The Death

A Peep at Christies ;—or —Tally-ho, & his Nimmey-pimmeney taking
the Morning Lounge.

8 Criticism and Review

Critics and criticism

'Tis hard to say, if greater want of skill
Appear in *writing* or in *judging* ill;
But, of the two, less dang'rous is th'offence,
To tire our patience, than mislead our sense;
Some few in *that*, but numbers err in *this*,
Ten censure wrong for one who writes amiss.

These lines are the opening of *An Essay on Criticism*, written by the poet
Alexander Pope about the year 1709. The *Essay* is a long work,
describing the not entirely satisfactory state of criticism in the writer's
own time and also – more important – setting down what he considered to be the most obvious reasons for its decline together with some
suggestions as to how the art ought to be practised. What's all this – you
may be asking – about *art*? Is criticism really an art? Is it really that
important? Well, Pope plainly thought it *was* important, that – as we
see from the first few lines of his *Essay* – it is less offensive for an author
to write rubbish than for a critic to lead us to believe that that rubbish is a
work of genius. Or, if we care to extend the argument and bring it up to
date, it doesn't matter if – say – a television company transmits a bad,
biased documentary programme so long as the reviewers and columnists
in our daily papers do not then proceed to tell us in a tone of great
authority that it is in fact good and fair.

   1   Do you agree, from your experience, that the critic has an equal if
not greater responsibility to his public than the creative artist?

   But again – you may be objecting – what does it matter? Critics and
criticism do not play so large or important a part in our daily lives – so
why all the fuss? Let us think for a moment, though, about what
criticism really is – the evaluation or interpretation (usually) of a work

of art on the basis of its merits, its effectiveness and its capacity for pleasing people. In public, this is generally done by men and women who are experts in their field, but in private it is a process carried on to a greater or lesser extent by each and every one of us. We may not write down our views, we may instead impart them in informal conversation with a friend. Nor may we devote our attention to paintings, poems or opera. But how often do we recommend each other — taking care at the same time to explain the reasons for our recommendation — to read a particular novel or see a particular film? How often compare our reactions to the programme we watched on television or listened to on the radio last night? How often argue about the virtues of a particular strategy or piece of play in the course of watching a game of football or cricket or rugby? For in doing all these — and other — things we are in fact exercising our functions as critics. The main aim of this unit is to focus your attention on formal, written criticism and review (a review is normally defined as a piece of brief, generalised criticism of the type we encounter in newspapers and magazines); it will be helpful if, before we get properly under way, however, we consider the enormously important role criticism plays in our daily lives.

2   Take any single day and prepare a resumé of the examples of criticism you meet in it. As well as the more obvious areas and those we have already touched on, do not forget the sort of criticism you encounter in your domestic, social and school life or the kind of commentary which we often find in newspapers and hear on radio or television in which some expert or other interprets events for us, including as he does so an evaluative observation on the matter under discussion.

What, then, do we expect of critics and reviewers? What special qualities of our own do we employ when we perform the critical function? The following are some of the virtues Alexander Pope looked for in the critics of his day:
(a) candour — the critic should always be honest and speak the truth as he sees it;
(b) good breeding — he should never use his criticism as a vehicle for cheap sniping or scoring points at the expense of those whose work he is judging;
(c) humility — he should never rate himself superior to his subject;
(d) expertise — he must know a great deal about the area of life or art in which he is practising his criticism, so that he can judge from as full a knowledge as possible;

(e) impartiality — he must not be tempted into prejudice or partisanship but always endeavour to judge every work on its merits.

3   We have left this list deliberately incomplete. Can you suggest any other qualities which ought to be considered fundamental to good criticism? Are there any traps or pitfalls of which a critic ought to be aware?

How necessary are critics to the world in which we live? At different times in history, critics have been set up as having roles of particular importance to play in life. At one stage, for example, they were thought of as the men and women whose job was to dictate good taste and fashion — they were judges or arbiters of how writers ought to work, composers to compose, painters to paint, and the rest of us to live. At other times, they have been seen as moderating influences, preventing extremism or excess in art, reminding us of the need for good sense in all things. A more modern view is that, while they have the benefit of expertise in their particular field, they should be regarded as expressing merely a personal opinion: if we read a particular reviewer regularly, it ought to be not on account of his infallibility but because, over a period of time, we have come to recognise just how closely his views accord with our own.

4   What do you believe to be the role of the critic in society today? What sort of power and responsibilities does the professional critic have? What do you consider to be the extent of your influence when you practise the art of criticism, however informally? What are your own best qualities or worst failings as an evaluator and interpreter of other people's work?

Personal reviewing

The most common form of criticism is the personal criticism that we undertake and encounter in our daily lives. Often this criticism is presented in an informal way when we are chatting to a friend about last night's television programme, a new record or a new book. It takes a more formal shape, if we are asked to present our views as a written report or review.

The basic aims of such criticism, whether it be presented formally or informally, should be to inform your audience about the item or event that you are reviewing, to convey to them its essential characteristics and to make clear what your own personal response to it was. For example, if it is a book that you have enjoyed you will want to say something about the nature of its quality, in order to whet your audience's appetite. If it is a film which you found disappointing, you will want to explain why it did not live up to your expectations of it.

Writing such reviews can be difficult. It is much easier to say that we liked or disliked something than to explain why. Frequently, both in conversation and in writing, people merely describe what happens in a book or a film, without managing to convey insights into the nature of the book or film, or an explanation of why they enjoyed or did not enjoy it. Unfortunately, it is not possible to present a ready-made formula to make personal review writing easy. Indeed if, when reviewing a book, you follow a set pattern, introducing in turn, for example, comments upon plot, characters, setting, viewpoint and style, there is a great danger that you will produce a stereotyped, rather sterile review. It is, of course, important to consider all the aspects of a book when trying to define the qualities that make it an enjoyable or a disappointing read. Often, however, you may find it easier to pinpoint these qualities by focussing upon a particular incident in the book and thinking about what makes it so interesting or exciting, so frightening or funny, rather than just by considering the various aspects of the book as a whole.

Here are three reviews, which were written by children aged ten and eleven for a reviewing competition organised by the *Times Educational Supplement*. They all received runner-up prizes.

'Bulldog Drummond at Bay' by Sapper

As anybody having the slightest experience of Bulldog Drummond will know, Captain Drummond is a slightly out-of-date bully. Nevertheless, he is not an ordinary bully. He is — after a fashion — a sophisticated bully.

In the first chapter Drummond is sitting quietly in his Nanny's house, minding his own business and bothering nobody. He is totally unprepared for a smashed window, or two midnight investigations!

Bulldog Drummond always keeps a weather-eye open for a city-bred damsel, in distress or not, and when a young beauty has a breakdown, well!

Miss Doris Venables is a key to an entirely illegitimate investigation of Der Schlussel Verein . . .

Der Schlussel Verein is, roughly translated, the Key Club, and five years previously it would have had nothing to fear from an investigation, but now . . .

Screaming, a 'pet' journalist in the cupboard, small daggers, murder, being locked in sound-proof 'how you say, ze doctor's room where he do things to people', and swapping 'hot' or stolen cars for some peppermint bullseyes: they all become regular features of this anachronistic yet witty and entertaining book.

Kerenza F. Gardner, age 11, Colston's Primary School, Cotham Park, Bristol

'Elidor' by Alan Garner

The novel starts when four children: Nicholas, David, Helen and Roland, were on the rampage in the streets of Manchester. They are trying to find something worth doing when they come across an old street map. They have a fiddle with it and decide to go to a small street called Thursday Street but when they get there they find that it is derelict. A mysterious old man 'magics' them with music into Elidor.

Elidor is a land which the powers of evil have virtually taken over but there is still a dwindling ray of hope left. If four treasures, a cauldron, a sword, a stone and a spear, can be saved and Findhorn made to sing, Elidor will see the sun again.

I think that this book would appeal to boys and girls of about ten or eleven years old. The illustrations are blurred and suggest a sense of evil about the story. When you get to the end of a chapter there is an intense force which makes you read on. There is some humour in the book, especially in a chapter called 'Paddy', when they meet an Indian bus conductor and a drunken Irishman.

The children are ordinary, not like the 'Secret Seven' and books like that. They argue, get agitated, cross and tired, while the 'Secret Seven' are hiring taxis, and agreeing with each other.

P. R. Brown, age 10, Packwood Haugh, Ruyton-XI-Towns, Near Shrewsbury, Salop

'Rosy is my Relative' by Gerald Durrell

Did you ~ver see an elephant that boozes? Adrian Rookwhistle did or rather had to see one! He received Rosy, an animal like this from his uncle.

Adrian, deciding the place for an elephant (let alone a drunken elephant) was a zoo or a circus, takes Rosy down to the seaside with the slight hope of selling her. All would have been well if Rosy hadn't upset the Monkspepper Hunt (lifting the master of the hunt in her trunk), spoiling the ball in honour of Lord Feneltree's daughter's eighteenth birthday (waltzing drunkenly with Lady Feneltree) and last but not least, stamping down a theatre while doing severe damage to the theatre owner. Thus, after this, Adrian and Rosy have to flee from the law!

It is a book that made me laugh so much that I could barely read. Gerald Durrell's description of Rosy slipping over the great polished hall, on the night of ball, letting off (under the influence of rum) gentle hiccups, smashing into the gigantic reception table and starting to drink some champagne that had spilled on the floor is guaranteed to give you hysterics!

> *Jeremy Lack, age 11, International School of Geneva, 62 Route de Chêne, Geneva, Switzerland*

For discussion

1   Which of these reviews do you think is the most informative?

2   Which review conveys most clearly the nature of the book?

3   In which review is the reader's own response to the book most clearly stated?

4   If you had to choose a winner from these three reviews, which review would you choose? Why?

For writing

Write a number of personal reviews on items chosen from the list of suggestions below. It can be helpful, when trying to define the qualities of a particular item, to draw comparisons between it and other similar items. Notice, for example, how P. R. Brown, in his review of *Elidor*, makes an important point about Alan Garner's writing by comparing it with that of another author, whose books he has read.

(a) A novel that you have just read.

(b) A television play or an episode from a television drama series.

(c) A book that you read and enjoyed in the lower school or any children's book that has recently been published.

(d) A television documentary film.

(e) A feature film that you saw recently.

(f) A new L.P. record album.

(g) A play or stage show that you saw recently.

Viewpoints

Work in groups and compile and then either video-tape or tape-record a programme called Viewpoints, consisting of interviews and discussions, in which the members of your group present reviews and opinions on a number of items from the above list. You will need to plan your programme in detail and to produce a script for the presenter. You can, if you are including reviews of books or records, also include extracts from the books or records to illustrate particular points.

Evaluative reviewing

When a scholarly book is published, the reviews of it that appear in newspapers and periodicals will generally be concerned to evaluate its usefulness and significance by relating it to the existing thought and theories about the subject in question. The reviewer may convey something of the content of the book, of its style and of the manner in which its material proceeds but he may also include in his review some direct discussion of the subject itself, so as to enable the reader to judge whether or not the book is an original contribution to the study of the subject. The following is a representative example of reviews of books on historical subjects.

Zig-zag Matilda

A review of '*Empress Matilda: Uncrowned Queen of England*' by Nesta Pain

Nesta Pain has chosen to deal with the bloody confusions of the reign of King Stephen, third down the Norman line from William the Conqueror. She handles them all in calm of mind, all passion spent, and this is quite a feat, because on no head ever did a crown sit more uneasily than on Stephen's.

Deliberately, she chooses pale phrases. Geoffrey de Mandeville, for example, as villainous a scoundrel and turncoat as ever clanked around on a destrier, she calls 'ever versatile'. Brian fitzCount, faithful adherent of the Empress Matilda, grand-daughter of the Conqueror by somebody else, was considerably less thuggish than the normal run of his contemporaries (which is not by any means to put him up among the saints in Paradise), and him she describes as 'an exceptional man in every way'. This is the cautious, two-edged kind of stuff which those obliged to write testimonials learn to reach for.

'A complex situation then developed' is another of her unexcited locutions – one indeed that might be taken as the leit-motif of her book. I am one who grumbles much about the grandmotherly government we at present have to bear with, as it pokes its unnecessary nose into this, into that; but give me the current troupe every time rather than be plunged into the marchings and counter-marchings, the casual slaughters, the seiges, the burnings of castles and crops – the total anarchy, in fact, which prevailed for the eighteen years between 1135 and 1153, during which Stephen and Matilda scrappily fought to decide who should succeed to the throne of Henry I.

In essence the struggle turns on whether the Angevins should, in the person of Empress Matilda's son, succeed the Normans on the throne of England. And in the end, of course, the Angevins did win, and Henry II did succeed, only to be plagued by Thomas Becket, most insufferable of men, whose patience, like Hitler's, was always being so quickly exhausted. Nesta Pain's antipathy to this turbulent priest gives, in the closing stages, a welcome vitality to a book whose tone up to then has been too anaemic to deal appropriately with a tale of unexampled violence and mayhem.

To be fair, though, it needs to be said that Nesta Pain is struggling with a central insurmountable difficulty: the character of Empress Matilda. Her apparent contradictions cannot now be reconciled: sometimes she is all tigress and virago, sometimes she is all weepy, womanly and biddable. The unimaginable touch of time has crumbled away the mortar building her personality and left a faggot of inconsistencies. Stephen suffers in much the same way: the centuries have dragged on, leaving him a faint, enigmatic figure flapping in the void his not very luminous wings in vain.

Walter Map, a generation younger than Stephen and Matilda, said of Stephen that he was 'not far off an idiot'. Well, that might explain him: indeed, it might explain Matilda too. The hard zig-zags of her life might easily have rattled a psyche much better balanced than hers.

David Williams from 'The Sunday Times' 19 February 1978

1   Where in this review does David Williams most clearly convey the issue that *Empress Matilda: Uncrowned Queen of England* is primarily concerned to explore?

2   In which sentence does the reviewer most directly state his objection to the book? Explain his criticism. Does he provide examples to support his criticism?

3   How much of this review is concerned with David Williams's own thoughts about the subject? For what reasons does he introduce them? How do they relate to the book he is reviewing?

4   Finally, consider the appropriateness of the style of the review, bearing in mind that it appeared in a Sunday newspaper. Why does he include references to 'those obliged to write testimonials', to Hitler, to 'the grandmotherly government we at present have to bear with'? Consider the effect of incorporating the final line of Milton's *Samson Agonistes* 'calm of mind, all passion spent' and the Shakespearean reference that follows it. What is the joke behind the title of the review? How do all these details contribute to the tone of the article and what do they assume about its readership?

Take a book, or perhaps a chapter of a book, which you have read as part of your own course of study. Write a review in which you discuss the subject treated by the book or chapter, as well as evaluating its contribution to your study of the subject.

The following review also appeared in *The Sunday Times* and is likewise concerned to entertain the reader as well as to evaluate Edward Heath's book. Of necessity, a review of a novel, or, as in this case, of a book of memoirs, cannot contain a scholarly discussion of the subject in question. The reviewer may, however, establish the grounds for evaluating the book by comparing it with other books of a similar nature.

Round the world in 80 clichés

A review of '*Travels*' by Edward Heath.
Ever since he left office, Mr Heath has subjected his public to a kind of relentless reminiscence about his pastimes. Bachelors are such singleminded hobbyists. After 'Sailing' and 'Music' we have

Travels and before long no doubt we will be privileged to witness Mr Heath signing even more titles about other chaste recreations.

He is strong on scrapbook memorabilia – this present book contains the newspaper articles he wrote decades ago for the *Advertiser & Echo* (Broadstairs), tourist brochures, holiday snaps ('The picnic we had on our way from Warsaw to Lodz'), a forty-year-old Spanish letter of authorisation, and ancient press cuttings. But he is weak on detail of other sorts. For a man whose second favourite word is 'particularly' he is highly unparticular. The word most favoured in this book is 'agreeable'. Bamberg was 'an agreeable place', Nairobi was 'pleasant and agreeable', and The Forbidden City? Mr Heath does not equivocate: 'Agreeable'.

There is almost entirely a record of happy days abroad, for however exotic or distant the place what Mr Heath requires is a good meal, a hot bath, a night's sleep, solid comfort – no crowds, no awkward temperatures (he always reports whether a place was hot or cold). His time in Venice is typical: he spends his time 'exploring different churches' – the churches are not named; he eats 'meals' – no dishes are listed; he stays at a 'hotel' – he doesn't say which one. And 'I was captivated by Venice'. I was not captivated by Mr Heath's Venice.

But travel writing is a funny thing. The worst trips, in retrospect, make the best reading, which is why Graham Greene's '*The Lawless Roads*' and Kinglake's '*Eothen*' are so superb; and the most comfortable travel ('There was invariably split-second timing and exact positioning as they drew up at the steps leading to the red carpet and the welcoming party') becomes in the telling little more than chatting or, in Mr Heath's 'Travels', smug boasting. 'I wonder how many people in Europe know about the Caprivi Strip,' Mr Heath inquires, and lest anyone mistake this for a Dutch fandango, he adds 'and how many people have been there?' Apart from the fact that he is saying 'I have and you haven't' he says practically nothing about the place itself. Like so many of his destinations – like Venice, for goodness sake – it is merely a name.

Mr Heath has been promoted as a man with wide interests. You name it and he has sung it, or sailed in it or been there. He is a statesmanly combination of Toscanini or Joshua Slocum, and now he is an indefatigable traveller. He laments that as an official visitor he has been unable to see much of 'the day-to-day life of the people'. And yet here he is in Kenya at the time of the Mau Mau troubles. He praises the chintzes at Nairobi's Norfolk Hotel, the carved doorways in the old Arab quarter in Mombasa ('The only attractive part of the town') and the coconut trees. In a twinkling he has had enough of the day-to-day life of the people and he is up the coast: ('I enjoyed excellent bathing'). In Miramer on the Mediterranean, 'I could swim and sunbathe all day', and on the little island of Gan, which has been the undoing of many an RAF man, Mr Heath spends 'a few hours bathing in the translucent light-green water.' I would be willing to wager anything that his next book is called 'Swimming'.

But is this travel at all? The Arab quarter is attractive because it has carved doorways and worthy of mention because it is attractive? If you can have a swim and a good snooze, yes, Mr Heath says, that's travel. And here is Aden: 'Aden was quite different. The colony existed largely to meet the maritime need for oil, as it had originally done for bunkering coal. I can remember little attractive about it.' Sometimes his bathing mania is spatch-cocked into a political judgement, as in this baffling and ungrammatical sentence: 'Durban was a fine city, though the purity of its beaches and the joys of its bathing were exaggerated, but the conditions of the workers in the sugar-growing area to the north were far from attractive.'

And you thought only his French was bad! Interestingly, he went abroad for the first time, as a schoolboy, in order to improve his French. He has been on the move ever since. His early trips, made under the name E. R. G. Heath, were to Germany in 1937 ('I knew then, without a doubt, that the crunch would come') and Spain in 1938 (Barcelona: 'Our hotel was comfortable') and again to France ('Meantime it was good to be lounging in a hot bath'). He went to America under the auspices of the Oxford Union and to Europe under the auspices of the Royal Artillery.

After the war, Mr Heath was very much a sponsored vacationer, and his holiday to end all holidays was his trip to China. He liked China. He clearly liked being treated as a head of state, which he was very far from being. His feeling for Africa remains ambiguous: 'I found, like many others before me, that once you have been to Africa the bug gets into your system'.

There is no question in my mind that this book is insufferable and badly written, simply another spin-off from Mr Heath's years in office. He has sold many copies of his other books, but as I fought my way through this one I began to wonder whether the people who buy them actually read them. I suspect that the book is bought to be signed, not to be read, and that the buying of it is regarded as a political act.

Paul Theroux from 'The Sunday Times' 11th December, 1977

1 Consider the structure of this review. It is much longer than the piece by David Williams. How does it progress and develop? How much is introductory and concluding remarks?

2 What is Paul Theroux's main criticism of *Travels*? Does he provide adequate justification for his criticism?

3 Where does he include general reference to 'travel writing' or to any other books of a similar nature? For what purpose is these comments included?

4 Attempt to define the pleasure that a reader of this review might be expected to receive.

5 Do you consider this to be a fair review of Edward Heath's book? Is there any sense in which the writer is exploiting his subject in order to entertain the reader and display his own wit? Need Paul Theroux have written at such length in order to make his basic points?

Look back to the list of critical virtues which Pope included in his essay on criticism and which appear in the introduction to this unit. Had Pope read the two reviews you have just studied, what comments might he have made about them?

Blurb versus review

If you look on the covers or jackets of most books, sometimes on record-sleeves, frequently in advertisements and on posters for films and plays, you will find a section devoted to proclaiming the merits of the work in question, encouraging us to buy or see it. This 'blurb' will often tell us a little about the theme or plot, will endeavour to whet our appetite by touching on the wit or pathos or suspense or excitement we are likely to discover in it. It may remind us of the author's (producer's, group's, actor's) earlier achievements, pointing out that if we enjoyed *them*, then we are bound to enjoy this latest offering. Sometimes it will go so far as to quote the appropriately flattering parts of relevant reviews. The idea, of course, is to sell the product – the whole venture is essentially a promotion exercise.

It is a far cry from the highly subjective approach of such blurbs to what ought to be the detached world of the review or criticism. Here, for example, is the blurb printed inside the dust-jacket of *Travels* by Edward Heath, a review of which we looked at in the last exercise. When you have read this blurb carefully, look back at Paul Theroux's review and then answer the questions which appear beneath the blurb:

Edward Heath has proved brilliantly his ability to share his enjoyment and understanding of two of his favourite pursuits – sailing and music. Both books were runaway best-sellers.

Travels will have a similar, if not greater, fascination for the reading public. It is a colourful and entertaining account of Mr. Heath's many visits to different parts of the world. It covers a lifetime's experience of peoples and places, ranging in time from his student days when he travelled in Nazi Germany and in Spain during the Civil War, to the tours made since he achieved high office.

Mr Heath is a knowledgeable, articulate and perceptive guide. He writes vividly about the countries he has visited, their peoples, the delights of their scenery and their artistic splendours. He also recalls his meetings with many world leaders – in moments both formal and informal.

In Mr Heath's two previous books the illustrations have been singled out for high praise. *Travels* is similarly and superbly illustrated. As before, many of the pictures come from Mr Heath's own collection, including some he took himself at a Nuremberg Rally and elsewhere in Europe, as well as in America before the war. Overall the illustrations cover a wide field, ranging from the Spanish Civil War to the beauties and wonders of the African continent, India, South-east Asia, Australia and the Pacific.

This is one of the most original travel books ever published.
from 'Travels' by Edward Heath

1   Are there any areas covered by the blurb that are not covered in the review? Are there any features mentioned in the review that are not

mentioned in the blurb? Can you suggest reasons for what you observe?

    2   To what aspects of the reader's interest is the blurb aiming to appeal? Does the review discourage him in any way?

    3   What comments would you make about the choice of words and tone employed (a) by the blurb-writer, and (b) by the reviewer?

    4   What, in general, can be learned about the different functions of blurbs and reviews from this sort of comparison?

    5   Does your study of blurb and review suggest that there is a danger in taking either of them (or both) too seriously?

Analytical criticism

Reviews of recently published books are likely to be very different from the more serious criticism of works of art which are already generally acknowledged to be great. The critic who writes about a great work of art does so in order that his reader might more fully appreciate all that the work contains and communicates. He will point out many subtleties in its construction and demonstrate how every small detail in the work contributes to its unity. He will, therefore, be *analysing* the masterpiece. The finest criticism of this sort is likely to be pursued, as Pope advises, in a humble and appreciative manner. The critic will have no intention of demolishing or devaluing the work of art but will seek to bring out every excellence that he can perceive so that the poem, painting, novel, or whatever the subject is, will become more accessible and comprehensible for others. His act of criticism will thereby sharpen his own and his reader's appreciation.

    This extract is from an essay on Grunewald's great painting of the Crucifixion, known as *The Isenheim Altarpiece*. As you read it through, keep referring to the painting, which is reproduced on pages 184 and 185. Discuss together all the details of the painting that have more meaning for you as a result of reading Huysmans' essay.

On the right of the cross there are three figures: the Virgin, St John and Magdalen. St John, looking rather like an old German student with his peaky, clean-shaven face and his fair hair falling in long, dry wisps over a red robe, is holding in his arms a quite extraordinary Virgin, clad and coifed in white, who has fallen into a swoon, her face white as a sheet, her eyes shut, her lips parted to reveal her teeth. Her features are fine and delicate, and entirely modern; if it were not for the dark green dress which can be glimpsed close to the tightly clenched hands, you might take her for a dead nun; she is pitiable and charming, young and beautiful. Kneeling in front of her is a little woman who is leaning back with her hands clasped together and raised towards Christ. This oldish, fair-haired creature, wearing a pink dress with a myrtle-green lining, her face cut in half below the eyes by a veil on a level with the nose, is Magdalen. She is ugly and ungainly, but so obviously inconsolable that she grips your heart and moves it to compassion.

On the other side of the picture, to the left of the cross, there stands a tall, strange figure with a shock of sandy hair cut straight across the forehead, limpid eyes, a shaggy beard, and bare arms, legs and feet, holding an open book in one hand and pointing to Christ with the other.

This tough old soldier from Franconia, with his camel-hair fleece showing under a loosely-draped cloak and a belt tied in a big knot, is St John the Baptist. He has risen from the dead, and in order to explain the emphatic, dogmatic gesture of the long, curling forefinger pointed at the Redeemer, the following inscription has been set beside his arm: *Illum oportet crescere, me autem minui.* 'He must increase, but I must decrease.'

He who decreased to make way for the Messiah, who in turn died to ensure the predominance of the Word in the world, is alive here, while He who was alive when he was defunct, is dead. It seems as if, in coming to life again, he is foreshadowing the triumph of the Resurrection, and that after proclaiming the Nativity before Jesus was born on earth, he is now proclaiming that Christ is born in Heaven, and heralding Easter. He has come back to bear witness to the accomplishment of the prophecies, to reveal the truth of the Scriptures; he has come back to ratify, as it were, the exactness of those words of his which will later be recorded in the Gospel of that other St John whose place he has taken on the left of Calvary − St John the Apostle, who does not listen to him now, who does not even see him, so engrossed is he with the Mother of Christ, as if numbed and paralysed by the manchineel of sorrow that is the cross.

So, alone in the midst of the sobbing and the awful spasms of the sacrifice, this witness of the past and the future, standing solidly

Napoleon crossing the Alps by Jacques-Louis David (Musée de Versaille)

Dedham Mill by John Constable (Victoria and Albert Museum)

188

upright, neither weeps nor laments: he certifies and promulgates, impassive and resolute. And at his feet is the Lamb of the World that he baptised, carrying a cross, with a stream of blood pouring into a chalice from its wounded breast.

> *from 'Trois Primitifs' by J. K. Huysmans, translated by Robert Baldock*

Study the other reproductions in this section or let each member of the group find a colour reproduction of a great painting and write as full an analysis of the painting as you can. Try to comment on every detail that you notice and show how it contributes to the overall effect of the painting. Discuss together the extent to which your criticisms enable others in the group to appreciate more fully these works of art.

You will have realised by now that analytical criticism is an exceedingly complex and demanding activity. Not only has the critic to hold in mind a host of observations about the technical excellence of the work and the arrangement of its details, but he has also to relate these more particular observations to a general interpretation, a sort of 'overview' of what all the details amount to. Consider this short poem by the American poet, Robert Frost. Try to work out your own interpretation of the poem before you go on to consider the criticism of the poem that is printed after it.

Stopping by woods on a snowy evening

Whose woods these are I think I know.
His house is in the village though;
He will not see me stopping here
To watch his woods fill up with snow.

My little horse must think it queer
To stop without a farmhouse near
Between the woods and frozen lake
The darkest evening of the year.

He gives his harness bells a shake
To ask if there is some mistake.
The only other sound's the sweep
Of easy wind and downy flake.

The woods are lovely, dark and deep,
But I have promises to keep,
And miles to go before I sleep,
And miles to go before I sleep.

Robert Frost

On the surface it is no more than a simple anecdote relating how the poet pauses one evening along a country road to watch the snow fall in the woods: 'The woods are lovely, dark and deep,' and as he sits in his sleigh gazing into the soft, silent whiteness he is tempted to stay on and on, allowing his mind to lose itself in the enchanted grove. His consciousness seems on the verge of freeing itself from ordinary life, as if it were about to dissolve in the shadowy blank, but his mind holds back from this. He remembers that his journey has a purpose. He has promises to keep and many miles to go before he can yield to the dreamlike release which the woods seem to offer.

This is the core of the poem, a moving personal experience exquisitely rendered. Yet in reconsidering it one cannot quite shake off the feeling that a good deal more is intended. The poem is not just a record of something that once happened to the poet; it points outward from the moment described toward far broader areas of experience. It expresses the conflict, which everyone has felt, between the demands of practical life, with its obligations to others, and the poignant desire to escape into a land of reverie, where consciousness is dimmed and the senses are made independent of necessity. There is no overt symbolism in '*Stopping by Woods*', and yet the reader finds his vision directed in such a way that he sees the poet's purely personal experience as an image of experiences common to all. The wide scope of the meaning becomes obvious in the final lines. These state the conflict in a simple, realistic way: the poet will have to fulfil certain duties, perhaps just chores about the farm, before he can go to bed; but the 'promises', the 'sleep', and the 'miles to go' widen to include more important aspects of his life and, further, elements of every man's life. Sleep here is, of course, the well-earned reward at the end of a day's work; but reaching out beyond this, as indeed the whole poem transcends its rural setting, the idea of sleep merges with the final sleep, death itself. It stands in contrast to the snowy woods, whose temptation is to an irresponsible indulgence ending in the loss of consciousness: it is normal death, the release at the end of a life in which man has kept his promises and travelled the whole journey through human experience . . . .

The wider areas of meaning seem completely taken up within the particular incident. This does not mean that the poem is the simple description it appears. One cannot dismiss the persistent feeling that more is involved, and indeed if the poem is read only as a series of flat, factual statements, it makes no sense at all. The fact that 'The woods are lovely, dark and deep' has no clear logical connection with Frost's next assertion, 'But I have promises to keep', unless one moves from the descriptive level to a more distant range of meaning and recognises that looking at the woods signifies more than idling too long by the roadside, the promises more than a few domestic duties. Otherwise the problem the poet faces would be too trivial to command much interest – he could while away ten minutes watching the snow fall and still get home in time to milk the cows. Similarly, the way the horse seems to wonder why the man has stopped is a trifling irrelevance if taken only as a descriptive detail; but it has the important function in the poem of establishing a contrast – one that continually interests Frost – between the merely natural and the human. The animal's inability to conceive anything beyond the practical concerns of food and shelter emphasizes the man's love of reverie and thus the sacrifices he must make to fulfil his promises. The reader, then, is forced to read the poem symbolically, whether he is conscious of doing so or not.

from 'The Pastoral Art of Robert Frost' by John F. Lynen

1   On which details in the poem has John F. Lynen specifically commented? Are there any other details that might receive similar comment?

2   What do you understand to be his interpretation of '*Stopping by Woods on a Snowy Evening*'? Do you find it a satisfactory interpretation? How has he arrived at it?

3   There follows another short poem by Robert Frost. Write your own critical analysis of it. Take into account all the statements in the poem and attempt to arrive at an overall interpretation.

Acquainted with the night

I have been one acquainted with the night.
I have walked out in rain — and back in rain.
I have outwalked the furthest city light.

I have looked down the saddest city lane.
I have passed by the watchman on his beat.
And dropped my eyes, unwilling to explain.

I have stood still and stopped the sound of feet
When far away an interrupted cry
Came over houses from another street.

But not to call me back or say goodbye;
And further still at an unearthly height,
One luminary clock against the sky
Proclaimed the time was neither wrong nor right.
I have been one acquainted with the night.

Robert Frost